# But You Look So Good and Other Lies

## A Memoir

Cher Finver

INFINITY PUBLISHING

ISBN 978-1-4958-1411-2



Published June 2017

INFINITY PUBLISHING
1094 New DeHaven Street, Suite 100
West Conshohocken, PA 19428-2713
Toll-free (877) BUY BOOK
Local Phone (610) 941-9999
Fax (610) 941-9959
Info@buybooksontheweb.com
www.buybooksontheweb.com

For Amaya

# Acknowledgments

Pat, this book is what it is because of you. Thank you for your time, patience, critiques, and your friendship. The world needs more people like you.

Stephanie, I am so blessed that our friendship has continued long after your wish. Thank you for your keen eye and encouragement.

To the few who read and offered feedback on my book before it was published, thank you for your input. I trusted you with the most vulnerable parts of me before I was ready to share it with the world.

Amaya, your many talents include makeup artist and photographer. No Spanx or filter needed.;-) Thank you for making me feel so beautiful the day of my photo shoot.

Adam, thank you for designing my book cover. I love the vision you had for it!

Lastly, to all my family and friends that support me (and I know there are a lot of you), thank you and I love you.

Some names and identifying details have been changed to protect privacy.

# Introduction

We all have a story to tell and I am no different. I've been through some shit...okay, a lot of shit. Those who know the basics of said shit tell me I should write a book, so I finally got up the chutzpah to do it. Writing is one of the few things I think I'm good at. I had a few small pieces published in the early 2000's and then I just stopped writing. I don't want to tell Saint Peter someday, "Hey wait, I'm not ready to go in. I never wrote my memoir!" I also do not want my great-great-grandchildren to know nothing about me.

I was born on January 9, 1975. My full name is Cherilynn but I go by Cher. Yes, like the singer. I was named after Cher although she spells her full name with one "n," not two. I have hated my name with a passion my entire life. I mean, can someone please come up with an original Sonny and Cher joke? And please stop tagging me on Facebook on the reminder meme to "turn back time" in the fall. I've come to terms with it lately and I do realize it is a good thing to have a name that people remember.

When I was two, my brother Tommy was born. I knew that his dad, Thomas, wasn't my biological father but he treated me as his own, so I called him Dad. We shared a beautiful two-story/two-family home with my grandparents in Medford, New York. Christmas mornings were always picture perfect with gifts overflowing into the next room.

However, my favorite memories were simply playing house with my brother in our huge backyard or running upstairs (where my grandparents lived) to watch *Three's Company* with Ba-Ba, my grandmother.

I had imaginary friends too. Willy Spaghetti went out for spaghetti (of course) the day Tommy was born and never came back, which I was apparently okay with. My favorite pretend friend was Nasha Ganena. I didn't talk to her, but I drew her and her beautiful sister, Kimberly, all the time. Nasha was ugly. Her hair stood straight up, as if she put her finger in a light socket, and I always drew dots all over her face. Looking back, I bet they were meant to be moles (or beauty marks as Mom called them), just like I have. Know that my hair has always been tamed.

I remember Mom briefly tried to go to college when we lived in New York. Tommy and I would knock on her bedroom door and we were often met with, "Go away, I'm studying." I adored my mother as most children do. She was beautiful, with dark hair, always sun-kissed skin, thin, and she was clever. This is why men adored Agnes too.

**Moving Day**

We were in the car longer than we should have been. This I knew. Tommy and I were thrilled to be going to Hersheypark in Pennsylvania. Being on a road trip with our beloved grandfather and our mother, whose attention I had always craved, was a bonus. When Agnes felt we were out of harm's way, she announced our true vacation destination. Maybe I didn't love chocolate as much as I thought I did (doubt it!) because I was satisfied with Las Vegas. We had been to Vegas once before and had stayed at Circus Circus, which is an exciting place if you are under twelve. There is a bargain Travelodge next to the Circus Circus and *that* is where we ended up this time. Don't think I didn't notice.

The orange comforter Tommy and I were sitting on was stiff and dated.

"We are staying here. We are moving to Las Vegas," Agnes announced. "What about my Barbie dolls?" I cried. "And my friends!" One question I did not have to ask was why.

Before moving, I remember bawling and screaming as I literally tried to climb up the walls inside the Suffolk County Courthouse in New York to get away. *Please don't make me see him,* I thought. I was so hysterical that he was promptly escorted out. I didn't want my biological father to find me, to take me away in the middle of the night from my mom or my brother. For these reasons, I accepted Las Vegas as my new home rather quickly.

My grandfather, Pop-Pop, stayed for a week until we were settled into a cramped apartment on the east side of town. One of the first deliveries I received from New York was indeed my Barbie dolls. At the tender age of ten, this instantly soothed me. Know that I played with my Barbie dolls until I was fourteen (the 80's were a much more innocent time). I missed people too, like my dad, Thomas, and my grandmother, Ba-Ba. Tommy and I would check in with the babysitter next door when we got home from school. We had cereal rationed out for us as a snack and often had breakfast for dinner, not realizing until I was older that this was because we were now poor.

Ba-Ba and Pop-Pop moved out to Vegas permanently shortly after we did. I adored my grandparents. They were always the calm in the storm of my life. My Uncle Richard followed with his family, but he was a storyteller and an abuser. So as quickly as they got here, my aunt and two cousins were gone. This made Tommy and me even more inseparable. Oh, we fought as brother and sister tend to do, but being the new kids in town, at least we had each other. And we had a secret to keep. No one could know why we had moved across the country.

# One

# Dirty Laundry

Dad moved out months prior to us leaving New York. I was watching *The Dukes of Hazzard* with Tommy when Mom and Dad came into the room and tearfully told us. If they fought, they hid it well. We were blindsided. Shortly after Dad moved out, we were sleeping over at his apartment. I woke up late to get a drink and I sleepily walked in on him and Catherine sitting on the carpet having a glass of wine. There was no time for introductions as I was quickly scolded and told to go back to bed. Catherine was also pretty like Mom. She had frosted tips in her hair (again, it was the 80's) and drove a Camaro. The license plate holder said, "Thomas loves Catherine" so you know it was serious. They are still married, so there.

Tommy and I were still trying to adjust to life out West when we were introduced to Sam. We sat awkwardly in front of the television while Mom rushed to get ready for their date. I did not need a new (step) dad but that's exactly what I quickly got. We came to Vegas in 1985 and two years later, my sister Angela was born.

"Why is she so dark? She looks like a hairy little monkey," I whined. She looked nothing like Tommy or me.

Sam was nine years younger than Agnes and just didn't know how to relate to me. God, I hated him. Who was this guy trying to discipline me? One time he tried parenting me and championed me to, "Get better grades now because when you are in high school, you can just relax and smoke pot." Sam always had a beer. Agnes spent most nights and weekends at Danny's Slot Country.

"I have to gamble to help pay the bills," Mom justified. I never questioned it.

We also moved every six to nine months. It was for my protection, I know, but that was a lot to be put on my shoulders. Changing schools often, always being the new kid in class. Thank God for Ba-Ba and Pop-Pop. He'd always get to school early to get that perfect spot to pick me up, and she'd always do my laundry and take me shopping. Their loving patience and time are the only reasons I have a driver's license today.

I didn't like my sister much, as it had been just Tommy and me for so long. Sam had a pretty bad temper too. He never hit me, or my siblings, but he could be a real jerk. I had a friend over once when he charged into my room yelling, "Can you not be so fucking lazy, and wipe your ass?!" He was holding a pair of my skid-marked underwear. Needless to say, I stopped having friends over much.

Catherine and Dad would send for us once a year, usually in the summer, and we would always go to the beach. When we started coming for visits, I noticed a change. Dad and Catherine treated Tommy differently than me. Better different. I can't explain it. I just felt it, and it made me feel so insecure. They had a decorative plate adorning their wall of a little boy on a beach that looked exactly like Tommy. They adored that plate. They always talked about that plate. I hated that plate. Where was *my* plate?

I walked to the dumpster with tears rolling down my face. How could I pack my life up into just two boxes and throw everything else I owned in the trash as instructed? In 1988, I came home from school and was told that Sam was joining the military. In El Paso, Texas. Huh? What? Unlike the move to Vegas, this one I contested, but what was I going to do? At fourteen, if your mom tells you, "We are moving," you move.

I was miserable in Texas. The only plus? Gone was the always-picked-last girl with the worst overbite you've ever seen. Let me introduce you to the teen with the hot body and cute face (with braces). El Paso is near the Mexican border and I was the only white girl in my class. That alone made me very popular for some reason. Sam could not get into the military. He ended up staying home and watched Angela while Agnes worked. This is when we were at our poorest too. As a teen, there's nothing more embarrassing than standing in the grocery line, paying with food stamps.

"You can only pick one big gift this year, Cher," Mom said. "Everything else will be stocking stuffers." My one big gift that year, a New Kids On The Block's *Hangin' Tough* cassette tape, was wrapped in newspaper.

Tommy and I dreaded walking home from school when only Sam was there. He was like a ticking time bomb. One day that bomb must have gone off because there was Mom, waiting for us as we walked home to take us back to Vegas once again. Of course, it didn't take long for Sam and Mom to get back together and he was back in Vegas too.

Mom would get upset at the extravagant Christmas gifts Dad and Catherine used to send us like perfume, money, televisions, and Starter jackets. She would say that she took care of us on a daily basis, yet their gifts always seemed to outshine her. As fun as visiting the beach was, we missed snow. I assume Dad also missed Christmas mornings with us too, so arrangements were made for us to visit during the Christmas of 1990.

I don't know if it was my idea or Tommy's but while Dad and Catherine were out, we played outside in the snow in our pajamas and no socks. It was no surprise I came down with pneumonia in my left lung. Tommy was fine and went home as scheduled. I, however, spent my 16th birthday in the hospital with 6:00 AM wake up calls to check my blood gasses.

"I don't want any cake," I whispered as I rolled my eyes. I was being a little shit. This I can now look back and easily admit, but I don't think I deserved what happened next. He just stopped talking to me. The man I called Dad from age two to sixteen just disowned me. I called. I wrote. I apologized. Dead silence.

"Make sure you ask Dad about me, okay?" I begged Tommy as he packed to go visit Dad the following summer. For the first time he was going back to New York by himself, which was an in-your-face reminder of my abandonment.

"I will," he promised.

He did. "I don't want to talk about your sister," I'm told Dad had said. Excuse me. Sorry, his name is Thomas. He was no longer my dad I guess.

I was always grounded, either for my grades, sneaking out, or talking on the phone after bedtime. "I know you're grounded but if you agree to go with me and your sister, I'd like to take you to see the New Kids On The Block," Mom smiled.

From the age of thirteen to eighteen, NKOTB was my life. I was so certain I was going to marry Joe McIntyre. I wonder if his mother ever got my letters pledging my undying love to her son? I had every poster, every doll, every album, every comic book, buttons, bedding, water bottle, shoelaces, you name it. Any dollar I had went to the New Kids. You are very welcome, Danny, Donnie, Jordan, Jon, and Joe.

After we moved back from El Paso to Las Vegas, we used Ba-Ba and Pop-Pop's address no matter where we lived so I finally was able to stay at the same school. Of course I wanted to go to the concert with my best friend, Julia, but I'd settle going with my mom and then four-year-old sister. Tickets went on sale for the New Kids on a Saturday at nine AM at Video Tyme. Remember video stores? I knocked loud enough so Mom would hear me.

"It's eight o'clock, Mom. Are you ready?" Mom and Sam went out every Friday and Saturday night. This was the one Saturday morning that I needed her to not be hung over. We got to the video store after ten. The line was around the block (no pun intended). We did get tickets — last row, balcony.

"I'll look for you way up top," Julia boasted.

The announcer's voice boomed over the PA system. "We are sorry to announce that due to an illness, Joe McIntyre will not be performing with the group tonight." I lowered my homemade sign, like Joe could have read it from the balcony, and I started to weep. Mom was in the bathroom with Angela who had thrown a tantrum during the announcement. When she returned, Agnes was in no mood to deal with a crying toddler and teenager. The concert started and I did my best to enjoy it.

A woman then spilled her Coke on my concert program and ruined it. I started to cry. Again. There was an argument about a replacement, which ended by Mom taking that Coke and pouring it into the lady's purse. We quickly left and found a security guard. I don't know what Mom said, although I'm sure she left the Coke purse story out. The next thing I knew, we watched the last few songs from the 8th row. Take that, Julia!

By the time I was sixteen, I had run away a handful of times. I would always leave a note, go to a friend's house, or I'd stay with my grandparents. It was usually because of Sam or fights with my mom over Sam. "What do you want? Do you want me to be alone?" Mom questioned.

*Yes. Be alone. Be a strong independent woman who doesn't need a man to support you or define you. A man who was a brilliant title officer, but for the most part, could not hold a job. A man you would constantly fight with and spend time in separate rooms of the house. Yes! Be alone instead of THAT!*

She couldn't.

Mom also told me she hated me. Those are powerful words to say to your child. I know I wrote an angry letter or two and wrote those words to her on paper as a teen, but is a mom allowed to say it? You can think it. Should you say it?

Ba-Ba got me my first job at a drug store called Pay Less when I was seventeen. She was their beloved change lady (we have slot machines everywhere in Vegas). Her recommendation alone was enough to land me the job. With my first ever paycheck, I bought Angela a Barbie Dreamhouse. I guess I was finally starting to like my little sister.

I used my time there productively to date two co-workers. John was my first serious boyfriend. He was blond and very slender but cute enough. "Hey," I casually said at his checkout line. I knew the next item he was about to ring up was enough to get him to talk to me.

"You like REM?" It was fun watching him try to remove the CD from those long security sleeve devices they had back then.

"I do." I really didn't (then).

I knew HE did and THAT was the important part.

I had sex once before, at sixteen. I had a friend who had a "cool mom," and she lied to my mom about where I'd be going that night. "Hi, Agnes... Yes, it's nice to talk to you too. Yes, I'll be taking the girls camping." If camping meant hooking up with a twenty-five year old model named Jeff who looked like a young John Cusack, then yes, I was camping. It was quick, uncomfortable, and guess what? He never called me again.

Other than my innocently asking what a "69" was in the 5th grade and Mom drawing me a stick figure of it (awkward), we never talked about sex. It was the exact opposite actually. Sex was shameful. At least masturbation was. Mom would catch me pushing my genitals up against our couch when I was four, and take away my Donny and Marie Osmond dolls for being "bad." When she caught me masturbating as a teen, she'd just slam my door shut and we never talked about it.

This was the same woman who had sex so loud with Sam that Tommy would come into my room crying, worried that Sam was hurting her. The same woman who had sex toys in her nightstand. Yeah, Tommy and I snooped. I had sex at sixteen only because my friends were all starting to be sexually active and I felt left out. How stupid was that?

John and I dated for six months. We'd go to the movies and such but our dates always ended with sex. I was his first and I liked that. "Why don't we ditch school?" I asked with a smile. I started ditching a lot in the tenth grade. I was bored and just didn't want to be there. "And go to my house," John said as he bit his lip. You know what we did that ditch day until his mom knocked on his door.

"John, you're home? I need help with the groceries," she yelled through the door. I jumped up and ran into a closet. Naked. "Yeah, Mom, I'll be right there," he tried to say calmly. Not only were there groceries, apparently there were other chores he needed to do too. I must have been in that closet for a good thirty minutes. Naked. He would often whisper, "I'm so sorry, I'll get you out of here as soon as I can."

Pop-Pop would already be waiting for me at school. Just then, John's mom opened the closet door. Did I mention I was naked? "I've known you were here the entire time. Get dressed and then meet us in the living room."

I called Sam, not my mom. I figured he'd be cooler about it, maybe cover for me since he was younger and all. "Sorry, Cher. You're gonna have to call your mom on this one." I did and she came to John's house. The four of us sat at the kitchen table not making eye contact. "Is this your first time?" Mom asked. I knew what she wanted to hear so I said "yes."

On the car ride home Mom told me three things.

"We will be telling Ba-Ba about this but not Pop-Pop. It would kill him."

"I'm taking you to the gynecologist on Monday."

"You are grounded and can't see John."

We went to different high schools, and by this time, he had stopped working at Pay Less, so not seeing or talking to each other for months was the death of our young love affair.

Next there was James. Ba-Ba loved James. He was a good employee, clean cut, and Mormon. Meaning, he wasn't going to further corrupt her granddaughter. James' mom, however, did not like me. For one, I wasn't Mormon. Some of the nicest people I know are Mormon, but she was the super judgy type. Two, the one time I went to church with James, I wore a blue dress she deemed was too tight, and paired it with my ode to Madonna big cross earrings. I felt like she was waiting for me to burst into flames. No surprise that James was also a virgin. Aha, challenge accepted! It took nothing more than my asking. Okay, now I get why his mom didn't like me...

I had never been to a school dance, so when I heard about the dance GR (Girls' Reverse - where the girl asks the guy) I asked James. Problem is, the girl also pays. If I wanted something, at the age of seventeen, I bought it with my minimum wage part-time paycheck. That wasn't going to pay for GR tickets, my dress, and a fancy dinner. I must have been able to steal a good two hundred dollars from the cash register before I was caught.

"Can you come with me, please?" His badge read "Loss Prevention." I admitted to everything. Pay Less did not file any charges, but I was fired. There was Ba-Ba, working at the front of the store as I was escorted out. Don't ask me why, but Agnes still let me go to that dance and Ba-Ba acted like I wasn't a thief. GR with James is the first and only dance I have ever been to. Shortly after that dance, I broke up with him. Too clingy.

By this time, Mom had been falling into a depression and was spending even more and more time at the casino. Tommy and I grew apart a bit in our later teen years too. We had different friends and interests. It happens.

Angela would bang on my door, begging me to play Barbie dolls with her. Sometimes I did and sometimes I would yell for her to go away. Once I had a boy in my room, and bribed Angela not to tell on me by letting her play with my treasured New Kids On The Block dolls. They were proudly on display in my room, and Angela knew she was forbidden to touch them. Not only did she tell Mom the minute she walked in the door from work about my visitor, she also lost one of the New Kid's irreplaceable tiny shoes.

"I'm pregnant!"

Mom thought the first day of my senior year was a good time to tell me this. I just rolled my eyes (I did that a lot) and grabbed my backpack. Combat boots were in style in the early 90's. I happened to have them on when Mom lunged at me for saying something sassy that I don't remember. Without thinking, I raised both my feet to protect myself, and she ran into my boots.

"You kicked me! You kicked me and I'm pregnant!" Mom screamed. She came at me again. This time Tommy stepped in front of her. "Mom, she didn't kick you. Both of you! Stop it!"

I did not kick her and I can't believe she would ever say I had. Sure, I wasn't thrilled she was having another baby in her 40's with Sam, but I wasn't trying to harm her or the baby. I have been slapped. I have been dragged across the floor by my hair cave woman style. Still, I have *never* hit my mother.

I came home drunk for the first and only time after a night out with friends. Sam was waiting up and ushered me into the bathroom. I've never been able to throw up quietly, and as I was hugging the porcelain throne, Mom came in, picked me up, and pushed me right out the front door. That's when a white truck stopped.

"You need a ride, sweetheart?" The driver obviously could sense my hesitation. "Tell me where you want to go and you can ride in the bed of the truck." It was late and that sounded safe enough, safer than going home anyway. Plus, this guy was clean cut and cute so obviously not a serial killer.

I ended up at the home of one of the friends I had just been out with. I stayed for a month, coming home only to pick up some clothes. I found all my stuff on the lawn in trash bags. My friend had a large and loving family. We'd sit together every night and read from the Bible, eat, talk, and laugh. Together. I soaked it all in. Is this what a family was supposed to be like?

I don't recall a conversation with Mom about it or any apologies given. But eventually, I returned home. My room had been painted blue and I was moved to a smaller room in the house, despite being the oldest sibling. Luke was born in March of 1993. The baby didn't fix anything. Mom and Sam still fought, and I still fought with Mom and Sam. One evening after yet another fight, a few months before my eighteenth birthday, I thumbed through the yellow pages for a private investigator.

## Two

# The Beginning of the End

I stopped ditching. Mom made sure of that. I had no choice if I wanted to graduate high school. I can still picture myself standing on stage at the Thomas & Mack Center in my cap and gown. It remains one of my proudest moments because it almost didn't happen. Pop-Pop had emphysema. It is hard to watch someone struggle with something we don't give a second thought to, like breathing. With time, it only got worse. He was at Desert Springs Hospital often, including the day I graduated. After the ceremony, we headed over to the hospital so he could be a part of my day.

After high school, Sam got me a job at a real estate title company. When I walked in, it was already known that I was the boss's daughter. Sam's reputation at home was the same at work. However, whenever asked by the gossip-driven secretaries, "He's nice," was always my reply.

I had no desire to be a mean girl in my adult professional life. I went from being bullied for having buck teeth, and being the poor girl who constantly wore the one Guess sweatshirt I got as a gift way too often, to bullying a girl my senior year to the point that a friend and I littered her neighborhood with signs calling her a whore and listing her phone number. I didn't want to be *that* girl any longer. *That* girl could be a real bitch.

For my nineteenth birthday Mom announced that she and Sam were going to help me get my first apartment. On the first night in my new place, I had to call Ba-Ba to ask her how to make spaghetti. I had no idea how to even cook pasta! At home during the week, meals were always prepared for us by Ba-Ba and waiting in the refrigerator.

We hardly ever ate together as a family. And being the teenage brat I was, sometimes I'd mumble, "I'll just grab a bowl of cereal." Now I'm a great cook. All self taught! Looking back, I wish I would had spent more time in the kitchen with my grandmother and less time sulking in my room.

Living on your own is expensive. I hardly had any extra money to go out with my friends and I hated that. We usually just cruised the Strip because that was free. It was on one such night that I met Brett. Brett and I had graduated from Chaparral High School in 1993 but I didn't notice he was in my graduating class. We met after high school through a mutual friend. He had an adorable smile and was so goofy it was endearing. It didn't take long after driving on the Strip for us to start dating. Like John and James before him, I was Brett's first. I obviously had a type back then. Virgins!

Exactly thirty days after I moved out on my own, Brett moved in. That's what you're supposed to do, right? Grow up, go to college or get a full time job and settle down. Thomas paid for Tommy to go to college. No one was saving for me to go to college. I had dreams of being a flight attendant, so when I was eighteen, I ordered a brochure from a flight attendant school in Florida. When I showed it to Mom, I think her exact words were, "Ha, ha, ha!"

"On our one year anniversary, you are getting me a ring, right?" I demanded.

Brett came home from the mall days later with one of those tiny boxes, leaned down next to me on the couch and proposed. Despite a drunken call from Sam one Saturday morning stating that he wasn't paying for shit, the wedding planning went smoothly. On my wedding day, I stood there looking at myself in the full-length mirror. *I don't want to do this,* I thought. Just then, he appeared to walk me down the aisle.

**Two years prior**

"I need to find my biological father," I cried. The P.I. asked me some basic questions, and within minutes had a number for my paternal grandmother. I remembered her! We'd take walks to Woolworths and we had the best tea parties.

"I'm only seventeen. I'm going to ask my grandparents to mail you a check. How much do I owe you?"

"Good luck to you, young lady. No charge," he quickly hung up. I sat there for a second. I knew what making that call meant.

"Hello?" answered the frail old woman.

"Grandma? It's Cher." She proceeded to say and cry my name a few times.

"I love you too. I want to talk to my father."

"I'll have him call you. I'll call him right now." With that, we hung up. I sat there biting my nails, not believing what had just happened. *Was I ready to talk to my biological father? What about all the horrible things he did to me? Mom was going to be so mad.* Just then, my phone rang. It was my dad.

He cried, I cried. He had gotten a lead that I was in Vegas but wasn't sure. It was a short conversation, as I was very cautious. I told him I had to tell Mom about our talk and that I'd be in touch. This was a rare night that both Mom and Sam were together in the living room. "I just talked to my dad." It was a relief to get those words out.

"You couldn't have waited a few months until you were eighteen?" This was Mom's concern.

We had moved from New York to Nevada because my biological father and my mother were in the middle of a custody battle. They had split when I was two. I was told that my father had more money than Mom and was about to win custody for this reason. I'd be separated from my brother and sent to live with my father. I was always told he bit me and threw pots and pans at me to get me to shut up. I was also told he touched me inappropriately. We had to move so often because Mom had to protect me as my father could have been looking for me.

I didn't care that he had hurt me. Sam was an ass and Tommy's dad disowned me. I yearned badly for a father.

Now I had one. Plus, I didn't remember being abused. What I did remember was going swimming, making strawberry Nesquik together, and playing with my stepsister.

My dad flew me out to New York. It was nice to be fawned over and it was nice to be the center of attention. "Do you have any questions for me?" Dad nervously asked. "No." *Don't be such a chickenshit, Cher! Ask if he touched you!! Ask if he bit you and threw pots and pans at you. Ask him!!*

## Wedding Day

"And who's walking you down the aisle?" Dad had come with me to finalize the last of the wedding details with the wedding planner a day prior to my big day. "My grandfather." I had never been so sure about anything in my life. The man who was always there for me would be giving me away. There I was, walking down the aisle in the chapel at the Harrah's hotel. I see Brett's mom (also wearing a white dress, mind you), my dad sitting rows away from my mom, and my little sister beaming proudly as my maid of honor.

"I do." I didn't. I was just doing what I was supposed to do. You know, grow up and get married.

We returned from our honeymoon in California to a letter from my stepmom. It was an angry letter and it destroyed me. "How dare you not have your father walk you down the aisle! When you danced with your mom, you two looked like lesbians!"

Brett wanted a mother/son dance with his mom. Pop-Pop made it down the aisle but could not get through a dance because of his emphysema. My Uncle Richard was there, Sam, my brother Tommy, little Luke, and my dad. "I can't choose! Maybe I can dance with all of them. Dad's only been back in my life for a short time."

"You can dance with me," Mom interrupted. The fighting lessened when I moved out so I agreed. That fixed having to choose between all the men in my life. So I thought. After I read the letter from my stepmom, I tearfully drove to my mom's house. I then collapsed weeping in her arms.

"Unbelievable, Cher. I hope you see now the type of people you are dealing with."

## Pop-Pop

Growing up, I'm embarrassed to say I didn't know the difference between God, Jesus, and Joseph. Mom would say she was force-fed religion growing up, so she vowed to do the opposite with us. My Pop-Pop was dying. My rock. One of my biggest fans. The man who would sneak me out for ice cream when I was in trouble. The man who made the corniest jokes. The man I loved and depended on most in this world. I was lost. I was angry. Why would God take someone like Pop-Pop? I needed him here. Didn't God understand that?

Pop-Pop had been transferred from the hospital to a hospice. Mom and Ba-Ba were stuck in traffic, so I walked down the long gray hallway alone. There was Pop-Pop. The man who, no matter how he felt, always had a joke and a smile, lying there sweating, trying to take his covers off, trying to communicate with me to no avail, and ripping the tubes out of his mouth.

I called for a nurse but no one came. *Where was Mom,* I thought, *I can't handle this by myself!* I tried to calm him down, and ran back and fourth to the bathroom with a cold towel. It was on one of these bathroom trips that I looked in the mirror and told God that I understood. I saw for the first time how much Pop-Pop was suffering, and I did not want that for him. "Okay, I get it now. You can take him," I told God. If He even existed. Pop-Pop died soon after.

Brett and I were going through the motions at this point. I didn't feel he was there for me when Pop-Pop died, but to be fair, I don't know what Brett could have said or done. Since I didn't really know God, I felt the man who cheered loudest for me my whole life was now just gone. I was inconsolable.

When Brett and I had taken our honeymoon, guess how much awesome honeymoon sex we had? Zero, zip, zilch, nada. I know I didn't have any interest in initiating anything. The sex was hot and heavy when we first got together but quickly fizzled. Still, Brett did not deserve what I did to him. We were married less than two years when the beginning of the end came. He burst through the doors at my work, grabbed all my credit cards, left the used condom on my desk with a note that read, "The real reason we are getting a divorce."

# Three

# Weighty Matters

I remember trying to lose weight for my wedding as most brides do, but I was still able to pull off a tight dress, and easily cut to the front of the line at the nightclub. This was despite the fact that I had discovered my new friends, Ben and Jerry, and had a pint of their ice cream more often than I want to admit. I was curvy, definitely not fat, but food was starting to give comfort and a euphoric feeling I had never experienced before.

Mom and Sam broke up and got back together more often than I can count. Luckily, I was out of the house, and missed most of that drama. My three siblings, however, did not. When Tommy did move out, he also started drinking and gambling. Angela spent almost as much time at my house as she did at her home, and Luke was luckily too young to realize all the chaos around him.

After working in real estate for a few years, I wanted a change and started working various customer service jobs. No matter what job I applied for, I was always likable enough to have gotten the position. This was the case when I answered an ad for an office manager for a shoe company in Vegas. There was me in the front office and there was Travis, who worked out of our warehouse.

Not that it mattered to me but Travis was 5′6″ on a good day. He was also very handsome, although he never saw that. At nineteen, delivering woman's shoes all day seemed like an easy enough job. All of the sales ladies at our stores adored him, including our top salesperson and Travis' mother, Rosemary. While making a delivery and picking up money from one of our locations, Travis was robbed. The cops were called and because he had a warrant for unpaid fines, he was arrested.

I bailed him out, and then I sent him flowers just because. Brett and I were making a lot of money for our age and I handled the bills. He never noticed the charges. "No one has ever sent me flowers before," Travis' face was flushed.

"Well, now you can say someone has." I smiled. I told Travis I was (unhappily) married. He didn't care. I was lying next to Brett. Same routine. Work. Come home. Have dinner. Watch TV. Go to bed. No sex. I grabbed my phone and quietly called Travis.

"You up?" I asked.

"Yeah. Some friends are just leaving."

"Can I come over?" It was midnight. There was only one reason I wanted to come over.

I was already out the door. "Of course you can," Travis said.

I fell in love with Travis hard and fast. I like to call it a crazy mad love, the whole universes colliding thing. Travis even tattooed my name on his hand less than a week after we slept together. After that first amazing night with Travis (he definitely wasn't a virgin), I sat down with Brett. He rather quickly agreed that our marriage wasn't working, and offered to go stay with his mom and stepdad while I kept our apartment for the time being. What I neglected to mention to Brett was that I was gone all night in the arms of another man.

A few days later, I had Travis over at the apartment. I do know I purposely hid that condom in the bedroom trashcan. Brett must have known something was going on to go look for it. I'll never regret falling in love with Travis. I'll always regret how Brett found out.

One of the most thoughtful gifts I ever received was from Travis. As a young girl, I wasn't allowed to have an Easy-Bake Oven. In the early 80's, this amazing toy was deemed unsafe by some parents. Agnes was one of them. I mentioned this to Travis, and he just showed up to my apartment with one. I had never been so happy to bake a cake with a light bulb.

A couple of weeks after we had slept together, Travis took my hand. I noticed he was shaking. He took a long drag of his smoke and blew out his words, "I'm addicted to heroin." *Ah, OK. This explained a lot, especially those long trips to the bathroom.*

In my defense, when someone is in the bathroom for a long time, you assume you know why and you don't ask questions. I went for a walk to clear my head. I hadn't even tried pot (yet) and I could easily count the number of times that I had been drunk. Heroin? That was the hard stuff. Do you know what I thought after my walk? *I can fix this!*

**These were written by Travis (age 19), early 1997:**

The last 30 days that we have spent together have been the best 30 days of my life. I love you more than anything and will always love you.

Forever loving you, Travis

Cher, I love you so much that I listen to every word you say. Normally, with my other girlfriends, I never cared or listened to anything they ever said. With you I listen to every word you say because I care about every word you say.

Love you always, Travis

Not long afterwards, Brett knocked on the door of my new apartment, a studio in the white people ghetto on Sierra Vista.

"Hi." He looked worried as I stepped outside.

"Thanks for coming over." I tried to look as sick as I could as he handed me the check.

"I wish you the best, Cher, I really do. I hope you get the help that you need." I closed the door behind me, smiling at Travis.

Brightway Rehabilitation Center was in St. George, Utah, about three hours from Las Vegas. I dropped Travis off in June of 1997, crying the entire way home. Hoping that his using would stop, and that he would finally become the man I saw glimpses of and loved with my entire being.

I had to lie to Brett and told him *I* was addicted to heroin to save Travis and to help pay the deposit Brightway required. I was desperate. I knew he wouldn't have given me the money any other way. I did write Brett a letter shortly after I returned home, telling him what I had done.

I was heartbroken to hear Travis relapsed once while in treatment for thirty days. Still, upon his release, I wanted to celebrate his short-term sobriety. My favorite place to be in this entire world is Disneyland, so that is where we went. I had just gotten a decent check from a minor car accident I was in or else I would not have been able to afford such a trip back then after separating from Brett.

"I'm not feeling so well. I think I have the flu," Travis moaned.

I tried to hide my disappointment. "Well, I guess we can stay in the hotel room all day," I said flatly.

"No, let's go to the park." It was nice of him to try but he shit himself in Mickey's Toontown.

As he tried to take a nap back at the hotel, I took his wallet into the bathroom and starting going through it. "What are these?" I yelled. "Why do you have all these pawn shop receipts?" Travis was always quick on his feet, like most addicts. "I was going to tell you. I have a gambling problem. I pawned that stuff to have money to play."

Do you know my dumb ass believed his story? When we arrived home, Travis went to run an errand and came back magically feeling better. I believed that one too. My studio apartment was "robbed." You guessed it. That robbery at the shoe store? Travis took the money, fooling the cops, our bosses, and he even somehow passed a lie detector test about the whole thing.

It's probably no surprise that my family did not like Travis. My sister was no longer able to sleep over. Mom said it was because of my new neighborhood, but that was a lie. I hardly saw anyone else either. My focus 100% of the time was on Travis. What is Travis doing? Is Travis clean today? Eventually the job where we met became a casualty of this too. That was okay because my real job now was taking care of Travis.

"I bet you won't marry me now that your divorce is final," Travis said to me. I knew he was struggling to stay clean. I didn't care.

"Is that a challenge?" I questioned.

We were married on 10/16/1997 at a drive-thru wedding chapel, deciding on Mickey Mouse rings from the Disney Store. We celebrated that night in bed with strawberries and a bottle of cheap champagne. I told Tommy first, and I guess he called Mom. I picked up the phone to hear her unenthusiastic, "I guess congratulations are in order."

I got a job as a wedding coordinator at a chapel on the Strip. We moved from my studio into a small apartment because I was now pregnant. Travis got on Methadone to get off the heroin. I smartened up and had him give me daily receipts from the clinic. His brother, Dante, helped us move in, and unbeknownst to me at the time, he was also battling drug addiction. I was unpacking some dishes when the needles that were taped under the cabinet over the refrigerator fell to the floor. Travis had simply been forging the receipts from the clinic.

"You come near my daughter again and I will kill you," Mom threatened Travis as we dropped off the last of his belongings to Dante's apartment. Mom and Ba-Ba then urged me to do something about the new life growing inside of me. So I did.

Tommy and his longtime girlfriend, Autumn, made sure to bring some towels so I wouldn't bleed all over his car. "Can I see the baby first?" I asked as the cold ultrasound gel hit my tummy. "We don't recommend that for a few reasons," the tech was sincere, so I agreed.

The bleeding wasn't really heavy until I settled in at Sam and Mom's place. I was lying on the floor in Angela and Luke's room, holding my stomach, waiting for the pain to go away, the physical pain. The emotional pain would take many years. Travis knew what I had done and he understood why. In the end, he didn't want a baby conceived while on drugs either. I was fired from my job at the chapel (another casualty) and began working in real estate again at a small appraiser's office. My boss, Rosie, had a crush on me and I used that to my advantage.

I took Travis back rather quickly. He would say he was clean and it was 50/50 if that was true that day or not. Mom was done. She had enough on her plate. Sam had cheated on her, and Angela was beginning to act out. Luckily Luke had Ba-Ba as she watched him during the day. His biggest concern at that time was when does *Blue's Clues* come on.

We moved from my studio apartment, to the run-down one bedroom where I found the needles, to a seedy pay-by-the-week shithole, to now being homeless. I had a car we slept in until the repo man caught up to me. That's when I started to work for Rosie. "I'm working to get back on my feet as you know, but do you think I could stay here at night for awhile?" I didn't dare mention Travis or what brought me to the situation I had put myself in. Rosie was kind enough to say yes. I would wait until the coast was clear, sneaking Travis in at night.

Now that I was working steadily again, I was able to save some money and was homeless for only a short time. José was a little old Mexican man who lived in North Las Vegas. He rented out a few rooms in his home for a small fee. Hey, it was better than my car or Rosie's office floor. Have you ever tried to freshen up every night in an office bathroom with just a sink? It's not ideal.

I should add that José was also a dirty old man, asking me for hugs and kisses all the time in broken English, and then holding on to me a second too long. I can handle myself and our door had a lock on it, so I didn't really care. I was used to being whistled at and stopped on the street.

Travis told me he was clean now. Many times it was easier on me mentally and physically just to believe it. Four months after my abortion, I found out I was pregnant again. This time, I would keep the baby. Fix the mistake I had made months prior.

"Hello?"

"Mom, I need your help. Something is wrong. I went to the bathroom and this jellylike glob fell out. I need to go the hospital." I was unable to find Travis. He was supposed to be at the DMV but wasn't answering my pages. I had to leave a message at the DMV for him with which hospital to go to.

"I can't. Autumn's dad just died," Agnes told me. I could tell by Mom's voice that she was upset, but I don't think that it was for me.

"Are you on your way to Autumn's house or something because I really need to go to the hospital?" I was staring at the jelly in the paper towel.

"No. I just can't take you." Now Mom just seemed annoyed that I had called at all.

With that, I hung up. José was home and he took me to the hospital. As soon as I showed my sad little paper towel to the nurse at the desk, I was ushered back. There I was told what I already knew. I miscarried. Travis showed up two hours later, I could hardly look him in his eyes. They were dilated of course.

Sam had cheated on Mom (again), and this time she said she had enough. In the early summer of 1998, I moved back to New York with Mom, Angela, Luke, and Ba-Ba. I told Travis to follow me to New York when he got his shit together. Ba-Ba moved in with her sister, Mom stayed with one of her cousins before moving into a small apartment with my two youngest siblings.

I went to stay with my Uncle Richard, who had moved back to NY from Vegas years prior. I loved my uncle despite the fact that he was a compulsive liar and he abandoned all his children. I loved that he was a lefty, like me, and a Mets fan. I've been a New York Mets fan since the days of Darryl Strawberry and Dwight Gooden.

I quickly got a job as a secretary. I also started buying essentials for a place of my own too, a small television, a nightstand, dishes, and so forth. I even put down a deposit for an apartment. All within a few months of arriving back to NY. Travis spiraled more and more into his addiction, not having me to answer to. I had trouble getting him on the phone some nights and even filed a missing persons report after not hearing from him for a week. I heard through the grapevine that he was staying with Dante in Naked City behind the Stratosphere. *That can't be good,* I thought, but I couldn't really do much living across the country.

"Do you know what time it is?" Uncle Richard was livid.

"I'm sorry, Travis doesn't remember the time difference. I'll speak quietly." Just then, my uncle grabbed the phone and hung up on Travis. We starting yelling, and that fight ended with my uncle pushing me against a wall and kicking me out.

'Mom, I know it's late," I cried. "Uncle Richard just kicked me out because Travis called. Can I come stay with you?"

"No, you can't. And don't call Ba-Ba either."

"What am I supposed to do?" I panicked.

"Figure it out."

I walked to the ATM and took out the last of the money I had saved. I jumped on the Long Island Rail Road going into Penn Station, and walked over to the bus station with only a backpack of my belongings in the dark of night.

"A one way bus ticket to Las Vegas, please."

# Four

# God Thought She Could Handle It

It took me five days to get home. Five days of no showers and not much sleep. Five days of sitting next to strangers, many of who got a little too close and were in more need of a shower than I was. Whenever the bus stopped, I'd leave messages for Travis. I fully expected him to be at the bus stop when I arrived home. He was not. I dug deep into the bottom of my purse for some coins. Sadly I didn't even try to call my brother, Tommy.

"Hi, José, it's Cher. I'm back in Vegas and I need a place to stay for awhile."

**Aug. 13, 1998**

Dear Cher,

I'm in the Henderson jail for burglary. It was really a petty larceny that they turned into a burglary. I was trying to get a couple pairs of pants so I could come out to NY. Please, please write me back with a phone number to where you are at. I have been calling and calling your uncle's house but he keeps hanging up on me. Baby, I'm trying everything I can to get a hold of you. Please don't leave me and I know you have every right too. I miss you and can't live without you. Please I need to hear from you, you are the only thing I live for.

Please contact me soon, or my mom with a number. I go back to court on the 17th for an arraignment. I need to hear from you so I know what to do in court because if I'm lucky and you will not leave me, I will strike a deal and give up all the drug dealers and every body else to go free from here and my probation.

Please don't let it be over, I love you so much and if I don't have you, I have nothing. I need to hear from you. Please let me know how to get a hold of you. Don't leave me wounded. I'm going to try to get my mom to get my property so I can get your uncle's address to mail you this. I'm nothing without you in my life. Please still be my wife, one last chance please. My heart hurts not hearing from you. I know I will never find or be with a woman as good as you are. Not knowing is killing me, also please don't just stop talking to me please. I hope to hear from you soon.

Deeply Loving and Missing You,

Travis

I didn't stay at Jose's for long. Tommy helped me move into a studio apartment near Nellis Air Force Base. It was just a bedroom and a bathroom, and I shared a living room and kitchen with my next-door neighbor. He was a trucker and never home, which was good. I was civil with my uncle, sending him money when I could so he could start mailing me my stuff back. I took the bus two hours each way everyday to go work for a real estate agent. Travis had violated his parole (stemming from a check fraud charge), and an arrest for stealing clothes at the Galleria Mall was enough to send him from jail to prison for eighteen months in September of 1998.

Here's the thing. He went to prison for me. I wrote out the bad check he was on parole for writing. The DA told him he wouldn't go to prison if he gave me up. He refused to do so.

I'm considered the stupid one in my family. Listen, we all have our titles. For example, once when I was checking my calendar to see if I was free, I had asked, "What day does Easter Sunday fall on this year?" The bad check I wrote for Travis, I wrote it in the winter, yet in the subject line I wrote "Happy Birthday" for some reason. Travis' birthday is in May. This was the red flag needed to have the check-cashing clerk call the cops.

**Oct. 8, 1998**

Dear Cher,

I miss you a lot. I'm doing fine. It's been really hard not being able to talk to you on the phone. This is the beginning of the first steps of changing my life. So I'll be able to come home and treat you like a woman is supposed to be treated. Because I know I haven't treated you with respect and love like I always wanted to. But I know my greatest downfall were the drugs. I know this will be hard on you as well as me. I have realized I was at a point of destruction.

I'm always thinking about you telling me that you will give me one more chance. I appreciate that. I can't express enough in this letter how much I love you and need you in my life. Let me tell you a little about what I've done for you. I've seen the dentist and she said I had great teeth as long as I stay out of fights. Not that I'm planning on fighting but I must tell you that all these dudes are giving me a hard time because they say I'm so cute. Ha-Ha.

Please don't worry about it. I think it's funny also. Just remember that I love you very much and I'm going to do my best to stay out of trouble so I can come home to you. I've also been seen by the doctor and all my test came back negative. He said I'm a very healthy young man. They made me an appointment with the eye doctor so I can get some glasses. I've been having trouble seeing sometimes.

We have finished all psychological testing so all I'm waiting on now is to be classified to the yard and that takes up to thirty to forty days so I'm still in the fish tank.

It will be very nice to see you once I get out of the fish tank because I miss you soooooo much, and love you even more. It's going to be wonderful to be able to hold you again and kiss you again and for more than half an hour. Here, visiting is 4 or 5 hours long so honey get yourself ready because I'm going to smother you with the love you deserve.

Once more, I would like to apologize for causing so much trouble in your life. I was blind to the real love you gave me. I will make it up to you. This will only make me a better person. Because I do very much want you in my life. I love you and hope to hear from you soon. I will write again ASAP. – Travis

I knew Uncle Richard was lying. UPS tracking numbers started with a Z. I knew this from shipping shoes when I worked with Travis. "Uncle Richard, it's Cher. I've left a few messages now. I still haven't gotten any of my stuff and I've sent you eighty bucks already. You need to call me back. With a correct tracking number."

My mother knew I had sent my uncle money. She knew he had given me fake tracking numbers and kept my money. She knew he lied about everything. She knew I was struggling to get by and I could have used eighty bucks, or at least my stuff back. "I don't want to get involved," Mom would say.

Tommy flew back to NY to visit with family. According to my brother, there was my stuff, sitting in the corner at Uncle Richard's place. It was Ba-Ba who ended up helping me. She gathered my personal belongings and mailed me one small box a month. Of course anything that could have been returned to a store was gone. Many years later when I saw Uncle Richard again, he did apologize but his apology did not come with a check.

In November of 1998, I started a job at a company that manufactured industrial immersion heaters. I applied for a part-time receptionist job, but within a few months, I was offered a customer service/sales position. I worked in an office with my boss, his wife, a guy in shipping named Paul, and two other salespeople, Sara and Ruelito.

Sara's time was spent working only as much as she had to and waiting for her two daily cigarette breaks. Ruelito (or Ro as I call him) was the go-to man. He handled all the hard accounts and harder questions. I was thrown into this job with just a few hours training. No matter how busy he was, Ro would always stop to explain anything I asked. He's the only reason I kept that job at first. Once I finally knew what I was doing, I asked for more responsibilities and was given the added role of collections.

I knew what it was like to be in collections by this point. Cars repo'd, credit cards maxed, bad checks as I've mentioned, skipping out on apartments, you name it. I did a lot to survive in my early days with Travis that I'm not proud of. For these reasons, I was good for this job. I wasn't judgmental. I would say, "Just send us what you can this week," and people often did. Our main office was in Ohio, and my contact when it came to collections was a woman named Sue. More on her later.

I finally had friends again thanks to my new job. I was so lonely for so long. Mom, Angela, and Luke were still in NY, and Tommy would tell me, "I don't call because you move so much and I can't keep up." Once Travis was in prison, my life with him revolved around saving gas money to visit and lots of quarters for the vending machine at the prison, and writing letters — lots of letters.

Travis and I started fighting over the phone often. He denied it, but he was jealous that I had friends and a life now. Still, I visited every week, continued to craft my letter writing skills, and sent forty bucks a month to put in his commissary. Toward the end of his sentence, he was transferred from the prison in Indian Springs to a work camp in Jean, Nevada.

"When you visit here, we can have more contact," Travis hinted.

There are no conjugal visits in the state of Nevada, but hey, I'd take what I could get. A few months into his stay in Jean, I gave him a hand job under the table. We weren't caught, until I wrote him a letter about it. Did you know prison staff reads all letters!? I was banned from visiting but luckily Travis would finally be home soon enough and with eighteen months clean under his belt.

That guy Paul from shipping was also a work friend who was in lust with me. He was unhappily married. I had a husband in prison. I briefly stayed with Paul and then Ruelito while saving for a better apartment of my own for Travis to come home to. Paul left his wife for a short while, and had asked to stay with me in that apartment.

He was talking to his wife on the phone when I came out from the shower only wearing my towel. I stood in front of him and let it drop to the floor. Paul was a good distraction. One I never told Travis about. I hate that I cheated on both Brett and Travis but it happened, and I'm here to be honest, even when it puts me in a bad light. If I'm going to call anyone else out here, I have to start with myself.

Mom moved back to Nevada in February of 1999. Angela missed me, Tommy, and Sam. Luke was also always getting sick, not being used to the colder harsher weather in NY. Mom was not happy about moving back to Vegas, she still complains about it to this day. She met husband number four, Lorenzo, while in New York, and after Mom moved back, he followed.

Lorenzo looks like a cross between Phil Collins and Jack Nicholson. I always thought Sam looked like a cross between Charlie Sheen and Matthew Perry. Lorenzo is successful and hilarious. I liked Lorenzo from the moment I met him. My mom is extremely likable as well when you first meet her. She is fun and outgoing. Qualities people are naturally attracted to.

Travis got ridiculously buff while in prison. I mean, what else was he going to do all day? I stayed at a normal weight by not being able to eat out much as I was always just getting by. Putting the money I did earn toward my new apartment, bills, and visiting Travis. The tormented boy I knew was no more. This Travis was strong— mentally, physically, and focused.

He was released in October of 1999. His mom, Rosemary, picked him up while I was working, and took him to the apartment that I had set up for us the best I could. Believe me when I tell you that day at work dragged on and on forever. Having him home after being apart for eighteen months was wonderful yet strange at the same time. We went out for a cheap steak dinner at the El Cortez and spent the rest of the night rediscovering that physical connection that made me fall in love with him instantly our first night together.

## The Year 2000

"Don't forgot to fill the bathtub up, so we have enough water, just in case," I instructed Travis as we were heading out for New Year's Eve. Remember Y2K? Look it up, kids! The world was nervous that every single computer system would fail. Therefore, many people took some stupid precautions. We ate such a huge dinner. To this very day, I have never been as full as I was that night.

I was content. Travis was clean and had gotten work right out of prison for a company that builds exhibit booths for conventions and I was happy at my job. My family (minus Ba-Ba who stayed in NY for a few more years) was all back in the same state. My life would forever change that March.

When I had that studio apartment near the air force base, I checked the mail one Saturday hoping I'd see a letter from Travis. I walked back and collapsed on the bed as the room started spinning. I closed my eyes, trying not to vomit. Moments later, I opened my eyes and I was fine. I thought, *that was weird,* but never gave it another thought for two years.

I was so tired. Actually tired doesn't describe how I felt. Fatigued, exhausted, even lethargic. I wanted to sleep all the time, so I did. I was also extremely dizzy. Then I noticed the left side of my face went droopy, and that I couldn't stop drooling on myself. Seemed as if every day I'd wake up and something else was wrong with me.

"Maybe you have Bell's palsy." People meant well. I first went to an urgent care, two of them actually. Both doctors told me I was just tired and needed to go home and rest. All I was doing was resting!

It was Agnes who suggested I go see an ear, nose, and throat specialist. I've been deaf in my right ear most my life, so a specialist in this field was nothing new to me. Dr. Jackson spent an entire day running tests on me that proved my dizziness was not just vertigo. "I'm referring you to an neurologist as soon as possible." That neurologist was Dr. Theuvenet. The next day I was sitting in her office with Travis.

I explained to her the many symptoms I had been having for well over a month now.

"Have you ever heard of MS or multiple sclerosis?" Dr. T. asked.

"No. Is that like Jerry's kids?" I was clueless. She smiled. "I don't want to get ahead of ourselves. Let's send you for an MRI." I had never had an MRI before. Thank goodness I am not claustrophobic. I was back at Dr. T.'s office the next day, this time with Travis and my mom.

Dr. Theuvenet tenderly told me the news. "You have MS."

I started to weep, in part because I had MS, but also because I was relieved to finally know what was wrong with me. Travis stayed strong. Mom had her sunglasses on, but I saw the tears roll down her face. I was numb as I started telling people, not really accepting it yet, I guess. A co-worker at our Ohio office had told me, "God gave you MS because he thought you could handle it." I thought that was the most stupid thing I had ever heard. What my MS did do was make me start to think that maybe the world didn't revolve around me. A major medical diagnosis will do that.

So what is MS? I'm not a doctor but in its simplest terms, multiple sclerosis is an unpredictable and incurable disease of the central nervous system that disrupts the flow of vital information within the brain, and between the brain and body. Myelin is the sheath-like material that protects nerve fibers. In someone with MS, the body attacks myelin, therefore, the brain cannot properly send signals to the rest of the body. The cause is still unknown and symptoms differ from patient to patient but can include fatigue (check), numbness and tingling (check), vision problems (check), dizziness and vertigo (check and check), and bladder issues (check).

I was in the throes of an MS flare-up, so Dr. T. ordered a five-day dose of IV steroids. A nurse came to our apartment and taught Travis how to administer it. He smiled gently at me as I turned the other way. I never like to watch needles go in. I'd always sing to myself, *"Jessie is a friend. Yeah, I know he's been a good friend of mine."* I was there when Travis needed me most. Now it was his turn to be there for me, and he was.

I asked Dr. T. two questions when I was diagnosed.

"Will I be able to have children one day?"

"Yes."

"Will I be able to walk?"

"Maybe with assistance but I believe so."

Days later, I was sitting there stunned. Shaking. Not now. "It will be okay. You can do this. Everything will be all right." Travis seemed pretty convinced. My mom was on her way over to check on me. "Should we tell her?" I asked as I stared down at a positive pregnancy test for the third time in my life.

My period was late but I thought that was just because of the steroids. I didn't want to tell my mom. I still had deep wounds from her not taking me to the hospital when I called her from Jose's house. In six short months, Travis had shown my family that he was a different person, but were we ready for a baby? A baby who had a mother who couldn't even hold her own toothbrush at the time, so how was she going to change a diaper?

Agnes asked Travis to help her unload some groceries. "You tell her," I whispered as he followed her out. "A baby! Cher, this is wonderful news. Of course you can do this!" Mom was happy as could be that I was pregnant. This time.

There can be something with the hormones produced during pregnancy that is actually beneficial to someone with MS. I had to stop the IV steroids once I found out I was pregnant, but over time, I did start feeling like my old self again during most of my pregnancy. I continued working, as did Travis, as we anxiously awaited the birth of our daughter.

Yes, we wanted a healthy baby but to be honest, all my heart has ever wanted was a daughter. I thought the universe would never give me what I wanted, so I convinced myself that we were having a son. I had only picked out a boy name for this reason. After an ultrasound revealed we were indeed expecting a girl, I excused myself to the restroom and cried "thank you" over and over again. It wasn't until we got back in the elevator that Travis told me the entire waiting room could hear me. I didn't care, that day was one of the best days ever.

Eating for two. That's the excuse and I used it. I ate all the time, whatever I wanted. I weighed in at just over two hundred pounds before we headed to the hospital.

I like Thursdays. I was born on a Thursday, and when I picked the day I'd be induced, it was on a Wednesday night so I'd give birth on a Thursday. Plus, I didn't want the baby born any closer to Christmas than she was already going to be. Pop-Pop's birthday was December 24th. I remember he'd let Tommy and me sing the "Happy Birthday" song at warp speed just so we could then turn our attention to opening presents.

Ba-Ba had flown in from New York for the birth and to stay with us for the first month of our daughter's life. I was in labor for twenty-four hours. I was so miserable and uncomfortable because I couldn't sleep. Only Ba-Ba, when she rubbed my back and head with her long nails, could get me to relax and catnap. Lorenzo stayed in the waiting room with Luke, as he was only seven at the time.

Angela, who had over the years turned from my annoying little sister to one of my best friends, was front and center, as were Mom and Ba-Ba. Travis was so nervous he was constantly taking a smoke break, or was in the hospital's cafeteria. Someone had to track him down when it was time. I should mention that Tommy stopped by to say hello just as I started to push so he was trapped in the room, whether he liked it or not.

Amaya Rose Johnson was born on December 14, 2000 at 7:02 PM. She weighed 7 pounds, 6 ½ ounces and was 19" long. Labor was long. Delivery was not. A few pushes while embarrassingly dry heaving. That was it. Angela was so fascinated with what was going on "down there" that my OBGYN had to nicely ask her to move out of the way so he could do his job.

Amaya was placed on my chest. We locked eyes and time stopped. I've never had a more perfect moment and I doubt I ever will. They cleaned her up and she scored a

9 on her Apgar test. See, she's been extraordinary since birth. I was exhausted from labor and delivery, so she was then given to Travis. He was a tough guy but in that moment, he was a weeping father.

Everyone eventually left and it was Travis, me, and the most beautiful creature we've ever seen. I was starving, unable to eat for over twenty-four hours now. "I want McDonald's please. Supersize it." Travis left. I told him to hurry. Not only because I was hungry, but what was I supposed to do with Amaya if she woke up?

I'll let you in on a little secret about Amaya's middle name, Rose. I told Travis we were naming her Rose after his mother, Rosemary. I lied. My favorite movie is *Titanic* and Rose is the name of Kate Winslet's character. Ssshhh.

# Five

# A Messy Life

Rosemary never visited Travis at Brightway. She didn't want to participate in family therapy sessions, she said she was more of a listener than a talker, and she didn't want to air dirty laundry. She did put some money on Travis' books when he was in prison, and I recall her visiting him there once, maybe twice. I pretty much lost all respect for her when Travis told me she would buy him needles back in the day. She said it was better than him sharing needles. If that's your justification, I guess you have a point.

Travis told me that as a boy, he'd come home to Rosemary gone at the casino and nothing in the cabinets but pancake mix. She wasn't a great mother. She put men and herself before her two sons. Still, Travis loved her. Amaya was four months old when Rosemary died of heart and lung complications. She was only forty-nine.

We had plans to visit New York the day after she died. We went because Travis felt that is what his mom would have wanted. Ba-Ba took Amaya for us so we could spend a few days in the city. We were at our hotel when Travis asked me the question, "How do you feel about weed?"

I had never done any drugs other than huffing car gas when I was in middle school on occasion with a friend named Leia. I knew it made me feel light-headed, but at the time huffing wasn't really a word in our vocabulary. I also had no idea at the time how stupid and dangerous it really was. I totally could have died. She also ended up catfishing me before anyone really knew catfishing was a thing.

She pretended to be this guy named Mike. At fourteen, I fell head over heels quickly with someone who often sang to me over the phone. Leia told me after a month that it was her pretending to be Mike. She was gay and had a crush on me and was hoping my feelings for Mike would turn into feelings for her. Once, when we were high, we fooled around but I was only experimenting. When she saw I didn't have feelings for her, our friendship fizzled, and she moved on to doing the same thing to other girls.

I was offered cocaine and pot as a teenager but as Nancy Reagan had taught me, I just said no. "Pot is not like other drugs," Travis explained. "It just makes you chill. I have no desire to touch anything else. I work hard. I'm doing really well, and I'd like you to consider it." He had a point. He *was* doing really well and he *did* work hard.

To be honest, I was curious about it. Plus, as someone with MS, in the state of Nevada, smoking marijuana was legal for (only) medical reasons at the time. What was a little weed going to hurt? Not only did we start smoking weed (once Amaya went to sleep of course), Travis taught himself how to grow it. And to my surprise, it did help alleviate many of my ongoing MS symptoms.

Weed also makes you hungry. We had Dairy Queen almost every night as my weight continued to balloon. We went to DQ so often that the manager gave us a calculator, personalized with the store's location and logo. That's when you know you go there too often.

We moved Ba-Ba back to Vegas when Amaya was four or five. After Pop-Pop died, she didn't bother going to the gynecologist. I guess I understand her thinking, but this would become a regrettable mistake. Ba-Ba had ovarian cancer that had spread.

She underwent chemo, losing weight, and her hair. She did it with grace and a sense of humor.

Ba-Ba never sat still. She actually enjoyed cooking for you, doing your laundry, or being asked to sew back on a button. She needed to feel needed. And she was, to most of us.

"Mom, sit down!" Agnes would bark at Ba-Ba.

"I'm just so annoyed with her," Agnes would complain to Angela and me.

Mom hardly ever took Ba-Ba to chemo. My sister and I did. Mom was always yelling at her. Belittling her. "How come Ba-Ba is so loving to you? She never hugged and kissed me like she does you guys." I couldn't answer this for Agnes. I didn't know Ba-Ba as a mother, only as my grandmother.

Travis had been diagnosed with carpel tunnel syndrome in 2004. Those few years as a carpenter and a welder had taken a toll. He underwent surgery but it was not a success.

For the pain, he was giving a prescription for Methadone. "It's fine. I'm only taking what I'm prescribed," Travis assured me. This is around the time I stopped writing and I'll tell you why. It wasn't fine and I'm not a good actress. Stress is a huge trigger for me personally when it comes to MS relapses. I was always stressed so therefore, I was getting sick very often.

Travis started selling our weed to buy more pills. We both started seeing a crooked doctor for pain management so Travis could get more pills. Travis needed them at this point to function. For Agnes' 50th birthday, Lorenzo took us all on a cruise to Mexico. Amaya stayed in the ship's daycare while Travis and I ventured into Mexico. I was hoping to sightsee, but our time was mostly spent at every local pharmacy within walking distance of the ship.

I had started working part-time for Agnes and Lorenzo's health care agency, while Travis often worked sixty hours a week. We had two cars, a nice apartment, and we went to Disneyland every year. Travis would spend the rest of his life trying to make up for that first trip we took. Amaya also wanted for nothing. Yet, I was back to enabling him and he was once again in the throes of addiction.

Before the health care agency, Agnes had tried to open several businesses that failed. There was the aerobics studio, when every woman was a wannabe Jane Fonda. The bright yellow embarrassing station wagon we had advertising Agnes and Sam's at-home auto mechanic business, and then there was the flyer business. Agnes recruited her children to litter cars in the unforgiving Las Vegas heat with flyers for different businesses. I do give her credit for her entrepreneurial spirit.

I turned thirty in 2005 and had an "aha" moment regarding my mother. She was just like Rosemary and I was finally ready to admit it. She always put men above her children and she was at a casino more than she should have been. It seemed everyone in our family was afraid of Agnes. I didn't want to be under her dictatorship anymore. By the time we went on her birthday-cruise, Mom being drunk at every single social event was the norm. As I was putting Amaya to sleep in our tiny cabin, Travis walked in, looking puzzled.

"Agnes just gave me her credit card. Told me to go buy whatever I wanted."

"Well, don't. Let me have it and we will give it back to her in the morning." I knew better. Granted it was her birthday-cruise, and a few drinks would have been in order. But do you know Mom thought her credit card had been stolen? She had no memory of giving it to Travis and telling him to go on a shopping spree on the ship.

"Mom, you drink too much."

"No I don't. You drink more than I do."

*I can count the number of times I've been drunk.*

"Mom, you gamble too much."

"No I don't. You gamble more than I do."

*If I gamble eighty bucks a year, it's a lot.*

Mom and Lorenzo went on another cruise, over the Thanksgiving holiday while Angela and Luke were still minor children living at home. Don't worry, Travis and I had Thanksgiving at our house for them, as well as Ba-Ba. The fact that she chose the cruise (instead of Thanksgiving with her family) did not sit well with me and I told her so. This was the first time I had no contact with my mother. It lasted almost a year. My grandmother definitely knew and understood why.

I mentioned before a woman named Sue at our Ohio office. We struck up a friendship working together, which led to her and her husband, Gordie, coming to Las Vegas to visit when Amaya was just a toddler. Because of the age difference, they could have been our parents. Travis and I weren't expecting much out of the evening, yet it turned out to be a really fun night. In Sue, I found the truest of friends and the mother figure I felt I deserved. In Gordie, I got the purest caring heart.

Sue and Gordie have had a huge positive impact on my life. They are Amaya's godparents and I lovingly refer to them as my "Ohio parents" or my "bonus parents." Family is who shows up for you and they always have. I only worked at that heater company for three years, and I am so lucky to have made quite a few lifelong friends from my time there.

Travis had stopped growing pot when we moved out of our apartment near the Sahara West Library, and into a new two-story home in Centennial Hills that we rented. Amaya was about to start kindergarten and the elementary school was also brand new. At the tender age of five, Amaya would hear and see Travis and me fight. She would also take care of me when I was sick (she'd been doing that since she was very little) and help me hide Daddy's pills so I could control what he was taking.

Travis was selling even more pills and started seeing yet another seedy pain management doctor to support his addiction and growing illegal business. And I let it happen.

Travis sighed, "I have to stop going to that quick care on Rainbow. I caught a glimpse of my file and it had a note of some sort from the DEA (Drug Enforcement Administration). I also have to be more careful about filling multiple prescriptions at both Walgreens and CVS."

I came downstairs once to Travis sleeping sitting up (okay, he really was passed out) on the couch. The gallon of ice cream on his lap had tipped over, melted, and was all over the couch, coffee table, and carpet. He was still holding a spoon and melted ice cream covered his chest. I stood in the kitchen just staring at him in disbelief at what he had become so quickly. Then I took my cell phone and snapped a picture, so I could prove a point to him later.

I was lost. Travis was getting worse every day. I hadn't spoken to my mom, Lorenzo, or my siblings in months, and I was always sick. This is when I surrendered to God. There had to be a plan here, maybe God could help me find it. We started going to one of those mega churches. Amaya and I went every week. Travis' average was a little lower. This was around this time that I finally understood what I was told upon my diagnosis. God did give me MS because I can handle it.

Gordie is a minister, and he was always there to discuss the Lord with me. "Instead of baptizing you guys here in our hotel room, maybe we can go out to Red Rock Canyon," Sue suggested on a visit they made to Vegas in October of 2006. I had to drive us out to Red Rock as Travis was so out of it. I tried to hide this fact from Sue and Gordie, but they knew. We walked until we found the perfect spot, a large open area surrounded by the beauty of Red Rock Canyon. Gordie did the honors as Sue lovingly looked on. Travis said he felt the Holy Spirit go through him that day. I hope so.

Afterwards, Sue and Gordie wanted to see our new home. We sat on our porch for a while as they peered through my dirty windows. I lied and told them that my house keys were back in my car at their hotel. I was ashamed of our messy house. I am very neat. Like undiagnosed OCD neat, but not at that time in my life. I was always sick and so overweight and lazy that I hardly ever deep cleaned.

Our office? A room filled with still unopened boxes and papers everywhere. Our bed? Never made. Dust? You could see it on the shelves. Clutter? In piles everywhere. Not like I didn't talk to Sue on the phone all the time because I did. They knew our struggles, but I thought if they saw my house, they would know how chaotic my life really was. Normally, I can't even go to sleep with dishes left in the sink.

I began to question some of what I was told about my parents' court case back in New York around this time. I just had something in the pit of my stomach telling me to do so. Just like finding the private investigator when I was seventeen, I happened to get the right person on the phone at the courthouse. "I can tell you from these records that no one won custody per say. There was one mediation meeting," the clerk said. That must have been the memory I had as a child trying to climb up the wall. Even though we weren't talking, I e-mailed Agnes about it. She seemed bothered I was even inquiring, telling me she couldn't remember every last detail from so long ago.

Travis thought it would be a good idea to reach out to my biological father for answers. I knew we had the right number when I heard his voice on the answering machine. "Hi. My name is Travis. I am now married to your daughter, Cher. She has some questions for you in regards to your custody battle with Agnes. Please call us back." He never called back.

**A month later**

"I'm taking Amaya to the party," Travis mumbled.

"Trav, what party? Amaya doesn't have a birthday party to attend today. Where are you?" I started to panic.

He mumbled some more.

"Put Amaya on the phone," I begged.

"Hi Mommy." She was calm as could be.

"Amaya, where are you? What do you see around you?"

"I see a stop light and a McDonald's."

"Okay, baby. Can you put Daddy back on the phone?"

More mumbling.

"Trav. Please bring Amaya home. Please!"

From what I could make out, he promised to bring her home. I hung up, and started cleaning because I do that sometimes when I'm nervous. Ten minutes later the phone rang again, it was highway patrol on the other line.

## Six

# The Last Straw

Travis had run his truck into a ditch. He did not have Amaya in her booster seat.

"Hi Mommy." Again, she was calm, not a scratch on her.

"Ma'am, do you know what your husband was doing up here?" The officer asked.

I didn't. There was definitely no McDonald's or traffic lights up on Mount Charleston. Travis was already gone when I got there, taken by ambulance to University Medical Center. I confessed to the officers Travis' addiction as one of them held several empty pill bottles in his hand. How did I let things get this far? Amaya could have been hurt or, worse, killed. Just then my phone rang again.

"Cher, it's Lorenzo. Is everything okay?"

"Yes. Why?" He wasn't in my life so why would I tell him about tonight?

"Angela got a call from Travis. She couldn't make out what he was saying, something about Amaya and she was concerned." Lorenzo had reached out to me a few times in the last year, trying to convince me to make amends with my mother. Still, I was not ready to tell him anything.

"I don't know what you are talking about. Amaya's fine, she's with me now actually." The next day I took Amaya to the hospital with me to bring Travis home. "Things have to change, Trav," I placed my head on the bed railing and cried.

I had hit Travis a few times during our marriage. There is no excuse for it, no matter what sneakiness he was up to or what lie he had told. "If you ever smack me again, I'm going to hit you back," he warned. As we pulled onto our street, I smacked him again as we were fighting over the accident. He didn't just smack me back. He punched me in the face so hard that my glasses flew off, landing next to Amaya in the back seat.

In that moment, I remember looking into his eyes and not seeing my Travis anymore. I started sleeping with a knife under my pillow, and he started sleeping in our office or downstairs. I was so desperate that I visited the website for The Shade Tree shelter for abused woman and their children, but I couldn't bring myself to make the call for help. Honestly, I thought I was above going to a place like that.

Believe me or not, Travis was the best dad his addiction allowed him to be and he was always extremely proud of Amaya. At the open house for her first school year, Travis looked around the room at the lessons the children would be learning that year and proudly proclaimed, "Amaya already knows all this." His addiction did lead to lapses in good judgment at times. The booster seat obviously, but also taking Amaya swimming way past her bedtime in conditions colder than I would have liked (even for Vegas). Then there's the time he let her slide down the stairs in a box.

He loved her deeply. That was never a question. He went to work every day for her. He worked all the overtime he could for her. What he couldn't do for her was get off the pills.

I was doing my best at rationing out what he took every few hours so he could make it through the day and not be sick. He nodded all the time. Nodding is a semi dreamlike state where an opiate user slips in and out of consciousness. I can recall several times in which Travis would tell me, "You and Amaya would be so much better off without me." I'd always tell him that was, of course, not true.

I came home from church once to find Travis meticulously cleaning the angel urn Rosemary's ashes were in. It was a beautiful urn and looked more like a piece of art than an urn. Travis had many tattoos, including one of that angel urn.

"What'cha doing Trav?" I asked.

"I wanted to give her a good cleaning." There were Q-tips everywhere. "I wrote her a note. I opened up the base and put it inside." Rosemary's death was very hard on Travis. I didn't give a second thought to his note.

On Wednesday, May 16, 2007, Travis turned thirty. I was in the middle of a relapse, so I was not able to bake him a cake. He didn't mind. We stopped at 7-11, where

Travis loaded up on his favorite Hostess treats, and we just put a candle in one of them. I had gone to the party supply store a week prior and brought all the "over the hill" merchandise I could find. Amaya enjoyed hanging it all around the house to surprise Travis. It was a perfect simple day in our less than perfect complicated life.

Before we moved into our house, I received a certified letter from Dr. Theuvent's office. It stated that she could no longer be my doctor or Travis' (Travis had started to see her in regards to his carpel tunnel). I tried calling her office several times to ask why but deep down I already knew why. Same reason Travis couldn't go to that quick care on Rainbow. The DEA was on to him so she had to cut ties with both of us. Dr. T. is a fantastic, caring, and knowledgeable doctor, so I was crushed to lose her.

Amaya's school was only a two-minute drive from our house. I dropped her off on Monday, May 21, 2007, and then came home to get ready for my new neurologist. I probably should not have been driving, but Travis was too out of it to help. My new doctor would spend a few minutes with me and then write me a prescription for whatever I asked for. Of course, I'd hand those over to my husband. I was rationing his pills yet giving him the prescriptions for mine so he could sell them. It made no sense.

"Where are my pills?" Travis demanded.

"I have to go to the neurologist before Amaya gets out at noon. I'll give you your afternoon pills then." I grabbed my purse and keys and slowly made my way to the front door. Travis ran and stood in front of me.

"I want them now."

"Trav, stop. I really have to go if I want to get back in time." When I tried to move around him, he moved to stop me. "Fine. I'll go out the garage."

By the time I got to the garage door, Travis was already blocking it. MS can make you weak and I was very weak. Talking was exhausting. Our back and forth from the front door to the garage was getting old. I kept looking at the clock. "Do you want Amaya waiting for me to pick her up? Please move or I'll slap you." Know this was no real threat. I could hardly touch my own nose with my fingertip at this point. I wasn't able to do anything quickly or with force.

He didn't move. I "slapped" him. Next thing I know, I was in a chokehold in our garage. As I struggled to breathe, I went limp as a child does, and he lost his grip as I had hoped. "You choked me!" I said. "Have fun detoxing in jail!" I cried as I took the phone and dialed 911.

The next call I made was to my parents' work, Lorenzo answered the phone. As we waited for someone to arrive, Travis accepted that he was going to jail. "Please don't let me detox in jail. Please, Cher, tell me where my pills are." I told him and he took off for them upstairs.

Mom and Lorenzo couldn't leave work, so they sent my sister. I hadn't seen my sister in some time. She had started dating a boy who was a bad influence. I wouldn't realize until later just how bad of an influence he really was.

The cops came and separated Travis and me. He was in the living room, and I was on our porch. I was asked to write a statement even though I could hardly hold a pen, let alone organize my thoughts, and express them clearly. I told the officers the best I could exactly what happened as you have just read it.

In the state of Nevada, if you hit first, you go to jail. Period.

"But I barely touched him! I'm so weak right now due to my MS. What about him? Is he going to jail?" I asked through my tears.

"We tried talking to a supervisor about this situation. We're really sorry, but we have to take you in. You hit him first, and no matter the force, that's the law," the officer recited remorsefully. I had no idea what Travis told the cops, or why he wasn't going to jail too.

"Well, can I make a phone call regarding my daughter? I need someone to pick her up from school."

Heather was one of the playground moms. We'd chat while our kids played after school. Her son and my daughter were each other's first loves. I tried to calm myself before she picked up the phone. "Heather, it's Cher. Can you do me a favor and take Amaya back to your house for a bit?" She did, and my sister promised me she would go get Amaya from Heather after she got off work to take her to Mom and Lorenzo's house.

"Ma'am, we are going to put the cuffs on with your hands in front of you." This was kind, as I was getting sicker by the hour. I was also hysterical and scared, as I had never been to jail. Their kindness stopped when we pulled through the gates. My strength was almost all gone and I could only muster up a whisper.

"Can I have a wheelchair, please?" I begged the officers.

"It's just a few feet, you can walk." I walked. Barely. I slumped into the first open chair I saw.

"Johnson?"

"Here," I said quietly.

"Face forward." The jail photographer took my picture.

"Face to the left," she yelled. "Nurse please, we need a nurse."

Once, when Travis was in jail, he told them he had HIV so he could spend a few days in the medical ward with a television, in his own room, before the blood test came back negative. I was sure to get the same. Hell, I wasn't even lying. "I have MS. I was hoping to go to your medical ward."

"Nah, you'll be fine." She spent one minute evaluating me. I was escorted to a solid cement door with a small window. Inside the room, there was a pay phone, a toilet, and benches. There were also other criminals. Four spread out on the benches and two were lying on the cold cement floor, detoxing. *Okay, Cher, be cool.*

"Hello." I tried not to whisper so I wouldn't appear so weak. No one said hello back. I then walked over to the pay phone and dialed Mom's cell number. My attempt to not seem weak fell apart as soon as I heard her voice. "You'll be okay. We are getting Amaya and your bail is being posted right now," Mom reassured me.

Our group kept being transferred from one cell to another. I was fading fast. One woman in my cell yelled for a guard, "Hey, someone in here needs help!" It took twenty minutes for a guard to open our cell, do another quick assessment of me, and walk out. With MS, you can often "look normal", but that is the farthest thing from the truth.

Lunch consisted of a piece of ham and a slice of cheese on white bread with a packet of mayo. The guard opened our door while an inmate threw sandwiches to each of us from the doorway. "Please don't throw mine. I won't be able to catch it." As I said those words, my sandwich hit me in my face.

At night we were all instructed to take off our clothes and change into our jumpsuits. At home, Travis and Amaya would have helped me in my condition. Here, no one cared. I did the best I could, changing as quickly as I could. "Hey, sick one. Walk in front. Everyone else follow her." The guard screamed.

That is just what I needed. A long line of angry woman yelling at me to walk faster, all while making fun of me. The guards did nothing. The only consideration I was given was a bottom bunk. "What is she? The Queen of England?" My cellmate snickered as she was forced to change bunks. I didn't sleep that night. As the lights turned on to announce breakfast, I heard my name called once again. *Thank God,* I thought.

The woman who had kindly called for a guard for me the day prior was also getting released. She was in jail for fighting with her girlfriend. When I was taken to jail, I did not bring my purse, so I had no money. A full day and night of crying left me beyond thirsty and she bought me an ice-cold bottle of water upon our discharge. Let me tell you that water has never tasted so good. I don't recall her name, but I want her to know I am forever grateful for her small acts of kindness. I sat on the curb in the early morning hours near Fremont Street waiting for Lorenzo.

Agnes was waiting for me outside when we pulled up to their house. I was now almost three hundred pounds. I was embarrassed of this fact as I struggled to get out of Lorenzo's jeep. Mom just ran over and hugged me. Anything we were fighting over just melted away.

I went inside to check on Amaya who was sound asleep in the guest bedroom. Mom poured some coffee as we sat in the living room and I relived the last year. Going to jail was my rock bottom. I could not be with Travis. Not like this. I deserved better. Amaya sure as hell deserved better.

I spoke to Travis the day I was released on Tuesday, May 22, 2007. "I can't believe you had me put in jail. Me. In jail! We are done Travis. You need to go away and get some serious help. Mom and Lorenzo will be taking me to come get MY car on Thursday at seven o'clock. Make sure you are home."

He didn't protest. "Can you bring Amaya? I want to see her."

"You'll see Amaya again when you are clean and sober."

# Seven

# A Love Letter

**October 27, 1998**

Love,

I never imagined working for a company where only women worked and then falling in love with my boss as we were hanging out as friends to dinner and other places. I always wanted to tell you that I was falling in love with you. I wanted to tell you but I knew you were married and I didn't think I had a chance. I certainly wanted to take you home and make love to you all night.

I don't know if you ever noticed but I used to watch you while you walked around the office. I also used to think how great it would be if you were all mine. I wasn't expecting to get bailed out of jail by you. The very next night was one of the most magnificent nights that I have had in my entire life. I knew at that moment that I wanted to marry you. You were that special girl of my dreams. You have had a way of making me feel so relaxed around you but I was cautious as I knew the circumstances of you being married so, at the time, I was scared I was going to lose you.

I'm so happy to be married to an extraordinary girl. I fell in love with you because of your great personality plus your intelligence and most of all your wonderful sense of humor. I've always loved your looks. Your beautiful eyes tell the true story of how loyal and compassionate you are. If looks could kill, I would have been dead already. I love the way you kiss and it is very special for me to know that I have a wife who will stick by her man.

I love how affectionate and passionate you are in the bedroom and of course how elegant you can be when you want to be. It amazes me how responsible you are. I plan to learn and grow by your example. Please don't ever change the way you are because in my eyes, you are the perfect woman and wife for me.

I promise to cherish you and protect you until my dying breath. Sweetheart, I mean every word I say. I feel I'm the luckiest man on the earth to have you. Baby, I'm going to close this letter by saying I love you for eternity.

Your husband,

Travis

# Eight

# Only Travis Knows

Thursday, May 24, 2007, we pulled up to the house and I saw my car was not in the driveway. *Damn it, Travis!* I knew it was not in the garage as the garage was filled with moving boxes (despite us being in that house almost a year) and the unfinished desk Travis was building for Amaya. Lorenzo entered first, calling out Travis' name. He then headed upstairs to look for him. Downstairs, there were pill and alcohol bottles everywhere. Take-out containers littered the floor and furniture was turned over.

What the hell had happened here since Monday morning? I may have not dusted as much as I should have or been too sick or lazy to open some boxes, but our home never looked like a tornado hit it. I also noticed something else. Rosemary's angel urn was not on the table next to Travis' favorite recliner. "He's not here," Lorenzo yelled from upstairs.

Other than my car, I had come home to gather some medications, clothes for Amaya and me, and her favorite stuffed animal. Once we grabbed these items, I scribbled out a quick note to Travis. *We told you we'd be here at 7!*

*That's my car you're driving! Call me when you read this. And thanks for leaving the house such a mess, I hate you.*

Piecing together what I can, this is what I know happened between Monday, May 21, 2007 and Thursday, May 24, 2007.

**Monday**

Mickey was one of Travis' best friends. He had recently moved from Vegas to Atlanta and Travis took it hard. I do know that Travis called Mickey Monday night (when I was in jail) and told Mickey he was going to take his own life. Mickey called 911 and the police were back at our home for the second time that day. Travis later left the emergency room against doctor's orders.

**Tuesday**

Travis and I spoke about me coming over on Thursday to pick up my car. He did not tell me what had happened to him Monday night.

**Wednesday**

Travis called Sue and Gordie, asking if he could move to Ohio and live with them. I had already spoken to Sue, she was aware that I had spent the night in jail and why. She told Travis that it was not a good idea, and that she'd have to talk to me about it first.

**Thursday**

At 6:40 PM, Travis was traveling west on highway 215 east of North Lamb Blvd. when he ran off the road, overcorrected, hit a traffic sign, rolling my 1997 Grand Am GT multiple times. Travis was not wearing his seatbelt, and was ejected and thrown far from the vehicle. He was pronounced dead at the scene and my car was totaled. Toxicology showed drugs and alcohol were a factor. A coroner investigator came to the address listed on Travis' identification card. No one was home. Cause of death was listed as multiple blunt force injuries.

I had loved Travis to death.

**Friday**

Lorenzo had left a message for Travis on our answering machine Thursday night after we left, asking to call him about my car. The coroner investigator got into our home using Travis' key when he was trying to inform me Thursday night of his death. He listened to that message Lorenzo left, calling Lorenzo back at work Friday morning.

My sister was acting erratic, ranting about Mom, and getting ready to leave. She too was staying at their house after leaving her good-for-nothing boyfriend.

"Lorenzo, it's Cher. Let me talk to Mom. Angela is getting ready to leave."

"Put your sister on the phone," he demanded.

Angela reluctantly took the phone. Then she got quiet.

"Lorenzo's telling me Mom is on her way here."

"Why?"

"I don't know, but he's begging me not to leave."

I thought Mom was coming home to talk to my sister, calm her down, and get her to stay. She walked through the front door, silently pulled up a chair beside me and took my hand. From her face, I knew before she told me. I felt sick, I was numb, and I thought about Amaya. She only had a few weeks left of kindergarten and would need to be picked up from school in a few hours. Mom and Angela would pick her up for me but not tell her anything. That would be my burden to bear.

I also thought about money. I was on Social Security Disability, but Travis was the main breadwinner at that point. I had stopped working part-time at the health care agency when I went no contact for the first time with my mother. "He has a small life insurance policy, through the Teamsters Union," I remembered.

Mom called them and got the information needed to get that ball rolling. She then called Tommy. I saw Tommy less and less over the years. The last time I saw him was at a Halloween party at which he and Travis were trading pills. To his credit, he was at Mom's house within the hour so someone would be there with me when Mom and Angela left to go get Amaya from school.

I was still sitting in the same recliner I had been sitting in when I was told Travis died when Amaya came running up to me and jumped in my lap. "Mommy, what's wrong?"

"Remember how we learned about heaven in church? Grandma Rosemary is in heaven. Pop-Pop is in heaven." I barely was keeping it together.

"Yes. I remember." Amaya said.

"Daddy. Daddy is in heaven now too."

That was all I could get out before I broke. Before I could hand her off to my mom, Amaya got me a tissue and told me it would be okay because we had each other. Amaya was upset Travis was driving with a suspended license, but she didn't really cry until the next day. I was still in that recliner when she climbed back on my lap and started to weep.

"Who's going to be my Daddy now?" she cried.

"Daddy will always be your Daddy. Now he watches you from heaven."

Later that day I was tearfully telling Angela about Amaya's breakdown. With a stoic face, my sister said, "Why didn't you say her new daddy was going to be Brad Pitt?" I started laughing hysterically. Then I felt a little guilty for laughing.

Angela and Travis were very close. They understood each other. She once wrote that Travis was more of a brother to her than Tommy and Luke had been, so I know her comment was not at all disrespectful. I needed to laugh even if it was at the most inappropriate time. I hadn't laughed like that in forever it seemed.

Don't die over a holiday weekend. In this case, Memorial Day weekend. That mega church we had been going to for months? The one in which we volunteered our time and gave money every week. I couldn't get them to call me back regarding a funeral to save my life. You'd think someone would be on call or check messages. I didn't step foot in a church again for years after this. Travis' death also caused me to become even sicker.

I needed IV steroids again like when I was first diagnosed. I dictated my eulogy for Travis to Angela who wrote it down for me as I was getting an infusion. I was always told that I had the most beautiful handwriting for a lefty. Unfortunately, my handwriting has never fully recovered from the stress/my MS relapse of 2007. Nowadays, I can only write out a few words before my handwriting becomes illegible.

I needed to go to our house. Mom took me there, and somehow I beat her to the front door where I saw the business card for the coroner's office. There was also a business card on the kitchen counter with many of Travis' pill bottles lined up neatly. This is how I knew the coroner was there after I was at the house Thursday night. I knew I hadn't taken time, or had the energy to straighten anything up.

Amaya wanted her own pillow. Mom went upstairs for me to Amaya's room to get it but she couldn't find it. I made my way up the stairs slowly. Travis' birthday "over the hill" cut outs still decorated the stairway. I opened up our bedroom door and I was overwhelmed by Travis' scent. I went over to hug his pillow. That's when I saw it.

"I found Amaya's pillow. Travis had been sleeping with it," I told Mom. This broke my heart. He had asked me to bring Amaya when we came to pick up the car last Thursday. If I had brought her, would he have stayed home to see her? Could I have then prevented the accident, or would I have just been postponing the inevitable?

I had another reason to come to the house. Where was Rosemary's angel urn? Mom helped me back down the stairs, and we started searching. I was worried that he put it in my car and, therefore, it would have been destroyed. I opened up the garage, and there it was, next to our trashcans. Mom picked up the urn, and we went back into the living room.

"I can't do it, Mom. Please open it." I needed to read the letter Travis told me he wrote to his mom a month prior. Mom carefully opened the base, pulled out the letter and began reading it.

**Monday 4/30/07**

To whoever opens this, I'm Travis E. Johnson, son of Rosemary Russo. The woman laid to rest inside here. I'm 29, married for 10 years, and we have a 6-year-old daughter. I work as a Journeyman in the Teamster's Union. My wife has multiple sclerosis (MS). All we have is each other. No family or friends. This is Las Vegas, people move away all the time.

We live pretty good – upper middle class but still I hope whoever reads this is a relative of mine and is well off. I'm just hoping some of the sacrifices I made did some good to better my future family.

I haven't got a tattoo in three years, I used to go bi-weekly. Politics, George W. Bush is President. Iraqi freedom is still going on. Stupid war. Just bomb the mountain where Osama Bin Laden is hiding and call it done. We have lost enough men. They don't want us there so why free them?

My family is very loving. Amaya (daughter) is VERY smart because Cher (mom) reads and helps her a lot. Plus she will grow up to be a very beautiful girl so she has everything. And my wife is the best, they don't get better than that. The one person I can trust and know will be there is her. Same with me. I would do anything. I would kill, die, whatever needs to happen.

Regards,

Travis E. Johnson

P.S. It is hot outside.

"Was that a suicide note?" I cried.

Mom paused. "I don't know."

I looked around the funeral home chapel to see my family and friends there to support Amaya and me. Not one friend or family member was there from Travis' side. Rosemary was gone, he hadn't had a relationship with his dad since he was a teen, and I had no clue how to find his brother, Dante. His friend, Mickey, wrote something that was read at the service by my sister, as was a letter from Sue and Gordie and a few others. I invited Travis' friend, Will. He showed up as we were all leaving, but he did come back to Mom's house. We watched the entire service together that Lorenzo had taped for me.

**My eulogy for Travis**

*My beloved husband was born on May 16, 1977. 20 years later in May of 1997, we met and fell in love. I was his boss and he took orders from me for the next 10 years. He dared me to marry him 6 months after we met and I accepted his challenge. Then off to the drive-thru chapel we went! In March of 2000, when Travis was 23, and I was 25, we found out that I had multiple sclerosis. Less than a week later, we found out we were expecting Amaya. I know many 23 year-olds would have run for the door.*

*For the next 7 years, Travis was a wonderful caregiver. He did the very best he could of taking care of not only me, but Amaya as well. I want to thank him for that. He would frequently work 60-80 hours a week so we could have everything and he never complained. His favorite places were Amaya and my favorite places. If we wanted to go to Disneyland, he always took us countless times. If he wanted to go to the Outback Steakhouse for a steak and I wanted to go to the Olive Garden – we were having breadsticks!*

*Not only was he an amazing caregiver and husband, he was also a wonderful father. He loved Amaya as much as anyone could love someone. He never told her "no". He was so proud of her, and made sure she had everything she needed or wanted. I know his legacy will live on with her.*

*Travis did more for me than I could ever ask for. Like Amaya, he never told me "no". Last September, we took a trip to Santa Monica pier. I was in a wheelchair at the time, and could not walk to the ocean to watch Amaya play in the waves. Travis wheeled me over a quarter mile in the sand. I still can't get over that. Travis also made sure I saw my idol Madonna not once but twice. He was elated to shell out $800 so I could be only 25 feet from the stage. Thank you for all you did.*

*Travis loved tattoos, piercings, tools, the History channel, and he never missed an episode of America's Most Wanted. (He was sure that one day he would see somebody he knew).*

*However, if I wanted to watch something else, he never told me no. After seeing my favorite movie, Titanic, in 1997 together, every time it was on TV he would stop and watch it with me. He would also play it for me when I was sick. This is why I dedicated "My Heart Will Go On" by Celine Dion to him. You should all know that even though Travis looked tough, he was just a big teddy bear. You should also know that he cried like a baby during Titanic and Steel Magnolias.*

*Travis, I know you are now safe, not in pain, and with your mom. We definitely had our good times and bad times. We unquestionably were there for each other through sickness and health, and now that death parts us, I know I will see you again.*

*PS: As you may know, Travis was not wearing his seatbelt at the time of the accident. Please honor Travis by always buckling up.*

My mom ended the service by reading Travis' letter. "This is not what it appears to be. It was written and put away for when the day came." It was nice of her to put it that way.

For many months, I wondered if Travis killed himself. He had tried to kill himself by overdosing early on in our relationship, prior to going to Brightway. In the last few months of his life, every day I heard, "You and Amaya would be better off without me." Then there's hearing from Mickey that Travis had threatened to hurt himself after I was taken to jail. I would cry to Gordie, worried Travis would not have gone to heaven if he had chosen suicide.

I had to obtain copies of the autopsy and accident records for Travis' life insurance. Did you know they make the family gather all that? Of course I had to read every word, including the witness statements. I also e-mailed the witnesses, thanking them for stopping, trying to help Travis, directing traffic, and so on. I asked them all to tell me what happened in their own words. Everyone said the same thing. He swerved and then he overcorrected, trying to avoid an accident.

He could have hurt himself in many other ways too. Why take my car and drive miles from home to do it? We knew no one in the area of the highway where the accident was. I believe Travis was being extremely reckless, but that doesn't mean he was trying to take his own life.

My sister, Sue, and a few others will tell you they tend to believe that Travis did kill himself. When he overcorrected the steering wheel, it was just an automatic last minute reaction anyone would have had. Also, when I told Travis he'd see Amaya again only when he was clean and sober, he knew he just couldn't do that.

I will die not knowing exactly what he was doing that night. Only Travis knows for sure. Those domestic violence charges against me? Dropped the minute my lawyer told the judge the whole story. Travis was one of the true loves of my life. Writing this chapter was very difficult as I have so many regrets and unanswered questions. I still talk to him sometimes, asking if he sees Amaya and agrees with the decisions I've made for her.

# Nine

# White Trash

Something was up with my sister. I knew the signs as I had lived it with Travis. She was moody, she spent too much time in the bathroom, and she was hard to wake up in the morning. When I expressed my concerns to our mother, she said, "I'm not going to violate her privacy and go through her bag."

"Then I will." So I did. I found tin foil and a spoon, and there was hardly any money in her wallet, despite us just getting paid the day before. Agnes and I sat outside with my sister to confront her. She admitted she was using heroin. I had just buried my husband weeks earlier. Now I worried I'd have to bury my sister.

Mom took her for outpatient help. She didn't stay clean. Once Luke and I tried to wake her up. When she wouldn't move, we stood over her with pots and pans and banged them together as hard as we could. It still took a good ten minutes for her to move. She'd blame her sleepiness on one of her medications, but I knew better.

After Travis died, I spent a lot of time with Luke at Mom's house. We'd watch TV together or play pool. I adored my baby brother, and he was a fantastic uncle to Amaya. My sister was an amazing aunt as well, until drugs entered the picture.

Mom called Dr. T.'s office and explained what happened with Travis. I was allowed to be her patient again, which I was grateful for. I stayed at Mom and Lorenzo's house until September of 2007. By then I saved enough money to get a two-bedroom apartment not far from their house. A lot of people gave me money after Travis died. The biggest check came from an unlikely source – Sam. Mom also offered me my job back the day we found out Travis had died.

The first time I slept on the bed again that Travis and I once shared was torture, looking over, and not seeing him beside me. I had to get used to that. My sister moved into the same apartment complex where I now lived, and for a very reasonable price, I sold Travis' TV to Angela. This was before everyone had a flat screen TV that you hung on the wall. This thing was huge. Travis loved it and was proud of it. We bought it in the early 2000's with our tax return one year.

Once I was settled in our apartment, I had a mission, and that was to inform someone in Travis' family that he had died. I had a small box of Rosemary's stuff, but I never paid much attention to it, as I knew it was filled with mostly costume jewelry. Then I noticed a tiny notebook. Rosemary had apparently kept track of everyone who ever owed her money. It also included a few phone numbers, so I started dialing. Most numbers were no longer in service but I got lucky on the last number listed. It was for a distant cousin.

I told him who I was and what had happened to Travis. He knew how to get a hold of Dante and Dante called me that day. As soon as we spoke, I felt like a weight had been lifted. Now his brother knew. That's what I had wanted since May. Dante said he was also now clean. "Can I have Nate call you?" Dante asked.

Nate was Travis and Dante's father who lived in Mississippi. Well, Rosemary didn't know really who Dante's father was, but Nate later adopted him. Travis had actually told me several times before, "When I die, do not contact my father."

"Yes, of course," I said. That was the right thing to do. I spoke to Nate that day also. The next day he was at our apartment. Perks of having your own plane. Yes, you read that right.

"I want you to have a copy of Travis' obituary, and here's the prayer card we handed out at the service." I gently placed these items in his hand.

He was just a dad. Mourning the son he hadn't seen since Travis was a teenager. We sat down and watched the service. Lorenzo had kindly reedited it to include pictures of Travis while "My Heart Will Go On," played in the background.

Afterwards, we went to lunch and decided to go visit Dante, who lived ninety minutes away in Laughlin, Nevada now. It was a good day. I remember on the drive back home Nate and Amaya were looking for airplanes and made a game out of it. I was happy Amaya got to spend some time with a grandfather and uncle she didn't know but should. They were a connection to her father, and that connection was important.

I still had Rosemary's angel urn. When she died, Dante said Travis should have it and keep it safe. Now that Travis was gone, I felt it only right that it go to her other son whether or not he could care for it. Dante protested but I insisted. I made sure it was securely packaged as I dropped it off to be mailed. When the clerk asked what was being shipped, I fibbed and said it was just an angel statue as I knew human remains weren't supposed to be casually shipped.

**Ba-Ba**

I had plans to take Amaya and Luke to Disneyland in October of 2007 when Mom called. "You need to come say goodbye to Ba-Ba." I didn't know any other thirty-two year old widows so when Travis died, I leaned on my grandmother. Not to compare the forty-something years Ba-Ba and Pop-Pop spent together to the ten Travis and I had, but still. She knew what that emptiness felt like.

Of course I wasn't okay with Ba-Ba dying, but it was easier on me than Pop-Pop dying for two reasons. One, I now knew God. Two, I felt I had told my grandmother everything I ever wanted her to know. A year earlier, I had written her this for Christmas. I entitled it "Thank You."

*Thank you for marrying Pop-Pop.*

*Thank you for always getting up early and coming over to watch me open Christmas gifts when I was little.*

*Thank you for taking me shopping for my first bra and for all the times you held my unmentionables until we reached the cashier.*

*Thank you for loving me through my teen years, and for a safe place to go whenever Mom had enough.*

*Thank you for getting me my first job.*

*Thank you for doing my laundry for way too long.*

*Thank you for telling me how to make spaghetti the first time I had to cook for myself.*

*Speaking of the above, thank you for your spaghetti sauce.*

*Thank you for staying with Travis and me the first thirty days of Amaya's life. I haven't slept that good since.*

*Thank you for being the only one who could put me to sleep with a back rub while I was in labor with Amaya.*

*Thank you for always loving Travis.*

*Thank you for being my biggest fan.*

*Thank you for showing me what it truly means to never give up.*

*I love you more than I can express. Love – Cher*

I had a moment alone with Ba-Ba.

"Are you scared?" I asked her.

"A little."

"Don't be."

"You have to promise me that you'll take Amaya and Luke to Disneyland as planned."

"I promise, Ba-Ba. On the way home, we'll swing back by."

Mom called on day two of our trip. Ba-Ba had passed away and I had to tell Amaya and Luke. Amaya innocently asked if she could go back to playing with the Disney Princess tea set I had just bought her. Luke took it hard. Ba-Ba and Luke were very close, as she had basically raised him.

"I hope one day you'll realize you will see her again. That's the only way to get through it," I encouraged Luke.

On what would have been my tenth wedding anniversary to Travis, I was back at the same funeral home, helping Mom make arrangements for my grandmother.

Christmas 2007, I put up our tree while Amaya was at school to surprise her. How was I going to do Christmas without Travis? He'd help me wrap all the gifts, and I'd stand guard in front of Amaya's door as he placed them around the tree. He had this ridiculous homemade stocking that we made fun of every year. I completely forgot about his stocking until I pulled it out of a box of decorations and burst into tears. I eventually pulled myself together when my mind wandered to Christmas 2006. Travis was so high that he'd fall into our tree, sending it crashing to the ground on at least three occasions. Every time I'd quietly pick it up and salvage the glass ornaments I could.

Meanwhile, Agnes would bring Angela somewhere to detox or to get her on Methadone or Suboxone. She'd relapse. Every time she did attempt to get clean, Mom would give her back her job, car, apartment, and worse yet, her paycheck. Repeat steps one, two and three over and over and over again. Mom and Lorenzo own several houses including a condo in another country, and at one time, three businesses.

"You need to put Angela in a rehab, and not just for thirty days. It's her best chance," I insisted.

They could have certainly afforded it, but no one ever listened to me. Angela and I both worked for our mother. When she relapsed, guess who picked up the slack? Me. Was I ever given a raise? No. Was I ever told thank you? Not enough. I picked up the slack because I hoped that in doing so, I would get my sister back.

Things with Nate (and his wife Janet) were going so well that I questioned why Travis wanted me to stay away. As my car was totaled in Travis' accident, Nate was kind enough to give me $2,000 toward my replacement. He also asked us to come visit for a few days in the summer of 2008, even offering to buy our tickets to Mississippi. This was before I got on Facebook, so I had to keep all my friends and family updated via the occasional e-mail. Including Nate, Travis' stepmom, Janet, and Travis' adopted little sister Wang-Min, whom he didn't even know he had.

Around this time I had enrolled Amaya in the Kohl's department store Kohl's Kid's Who Care Scholarship Program. They offer scholarships for kids who do volunteer work. Back in 2005, I started volunteering for Make-A-Wish® of Southern Nevada. I mainly volunteered as a wish grantor. Another volunteer and I would meet with the wish child and their family and work with the office to make that child's wish come true. I would also volunteer at events and at the Make-A-Wish® office. Amaya was nicknamed "Littlest Volunteer," because beginning at the age of four, she would help at events and in the office.

Make-A-Wish® was my solace during my toughest years with Travis. I'd frequently volunteer thirty hours a month to keep myself preoccupied. Walk into a wish family's home and your problems don't seem so big. At seven, Amaya didn't win a scholarship, but she did win a fifty-dollar gift card to Kohl's. Amaya was excited to shop for her upcoming trip to visit Nate.

**E-mail sent by Cher to Janet on 6/11/2008**

Amaya's $50 gift card came from Kohl's, and it's so funny how concerned she was with the price of things knowing it was coming out of her winnings. Here's what she got:

Bathing Suit
Sunglasses
Tank Top
Shorts
Nightgown
Polly Pocket & a water balloon toy
*High School Musical* pop-up hamper

She shopped like a pro. Must run in the family. I did appreciate that on her own she bought stuff for her upcoming vacation and something to keep her room clean. Good girl!

**Response from Janet, 6/12/2008**

Cher needs to get a life. Do all these people really care??????

Janet meant to send this to Nate. Not me. She sent two apology e-mails in which she blamed her e-mail on being swamped at work, being stressed out, trying to get everything in order for the upcoming vacation, a foot condition, and red tape for said foot condition.

**E-mail sent by Cher to Janet, dated 6/12/2008**

Janet,

I got all your e-mails and saw that you called several times before I left for the day but I feel you can't take back what you said. I'm guessing you accidentally hit reply instead of messaging Nate. I am not mad. I am deeply hurt.

With all the red tape I had to go through relating to my MS or Travis, out of that frustration, I never said or thought what you wrote about anyone.

If you were so tired or overwhelmed with work/upcoming vacation, why then did you even take the time to write at all?

You are right though – Amaya is my life and I'm proud of that. Doesn't every mother feel their kid is their life?

Amaya and I have been through a lot. I'm proud of her for overcoming everything she has and that she is doing well. Not only is she doing well but that she still cares to do things for others – hence the scholarship e-mail.

I thought I was only sending the Kohl's e-mail to family and friends who cared and who asked what she got with her "winnings." When you and Nate sent me a copy of a poem Wang-Min had published, I did not say to myself "get a life, who cares?" I hung it on my refrigerator.

Travis NEVER had a bad word to say about you. This is all very tragic.

Nate is welcome to visit Amaya anytime he wants. I do not want to go to the Gulf Coast and spend four days with anyone who doesn't cherish me, or my child. I have so many family and friends here that do care.

Amaya and I were looking forward to coming, but now I know that I would be uncomfortable, so we are not coming. I won't tell Amaya the real reason either. I will blame it on the weather. I don't want her to think anything is her fault. Let Nate know that if he needs a letter from my doctor or something to get a refund for the tickets. I'd be happy to get it.

Don't worry – I will never again send you an e-mail relating to Amaya. I'm sorry for you that you won't really get a chance to know her because she's even more wonderful in person.

Again, you don't get to take what you said back and I believe you are only sorry that the e-mail was sent to me, and not for what you wrote. There is nothing you can do or say to make me feel any different. – Cher

Angela e-mailed Janet as well as she wouldn't stop calling and e-mailing me. This is when Nate got involved, asking me to reconsider my decision not to come. His excuses for his wife? "Janet is turning into her mother...she blurts out inappropriate phrases..." Mom then e-mailed Nate, asking him to give me some time. Nate and Janet continued to e-mail and call, offering to have Janet stay home if we visited.

**E-mail sent by Cher to Janet (cc: Nate), dated 6/12/2008**

I got your latest e-mail. I really wanted to be done talking about this today but no one seems to want to respect that. I'm not e-mailing anymore about this and I certainly don't want to talk on the phone about this. Please.

I'm sure you are sorry. Sorry the e-mail was sent to me instead of Nate, and sorry for any repercussions that e-mail will have for you w/your family. I didn't send the e-mail, you did. Maybe it wasn't his intention but Nate made me feel guilty by bringing up the money (gift) to replace my car, and for the money spent on airline tickets. As I said before, my doctor would be happy to write a statement stating I couldn't fly. I've NEVER asked for anything from you guys.

Bottom line is this - I don't feel comfortable, and I'm hurt. What would we talk about for 4 days? I certainly don't want to talk to you about Amaya or Travis. I'd be thinking the whole time that you are thinking I need to get a life and that no one cares. Maybe one day I can forgive but not by next week. You not going to the Gulf Coast or offering to get Amaya and me a separate hotel room only puts a Band-Aid on the situation.

I'm not trying to punish/disappoint anyone. My main goal in my Amaya-consumed-life is NOT to ever disappoint her.

Nate can come see her tomorrow if he wants. I think it is important he is in Amaya's life – to whatever capacity he wants to be.

Travis made it clear to me that he rather not have any of his family in Amaya's life, but any issues Nate and Travis had were between them and a long time ago and from the little I do know of Nate, he's been wonderful.

Amaya already knows we aren't going and I did blame it on the weather. I told her Grandpa Nate and Wang-Min may be seeing her soon, and she was okay with that. I told her I'd take her somewhere special instead of Mississippi and she said, "Cool, what's for dinner?"

I just can't accept your apology now. Sorry. I can't accept that you were having a bad day and just snapped or any of the other excuses. – Cher

**E-mail from Nate to Cher, dated 6/12/2008**

You know what?? I feel you don't have the class to step up to the situation. Amaya is definitely important to me, but it's going to take a few years before we know each other. If you don't bad mouth us. I'm sorry you can't work much and be a productive American. If you are going to be a vindictive person, screw off!!! WHY ARE YOU TAKING THIS OUT ON WANG-MIN

AND ME??? Yes, Travis and I had problems. He was a self-centered ass. Totally self-centered!!! He was a thief!!! You were married to him, you should know. Didn't he kick you when you were down? Seems like this is all about you, and that is wrong!!! I was not trying to make you feel guilty, but we did come to the rescue. Next time not! Las Vegas Trash!

I am so sorry for Amaya.

Your tickets have been cancelled. - Nate

**E-mail to Nate from Cher, dated 6/13/2008**

Wow. Thank you so much for that e-mail. It really showed me your true colors and the e-mail yesterday has shown me Janet's. Now I'm 100% sure that I made the right decision for both Amaya and me not to come.

I won't have to bad-mouth any of you to Amaya. She can just read all these e-mails one day and make a decision for herself. I didn't say one bad word about you. Not one. Like all of us, Travis was not perfect, but you had not known him for many years. The fact that you would also write any of that about your son who is now dead blows my mind.

I won't even comment on your "productive American" comment. You are all a real class act. I'm glad to know there is white trash throughout this great country.

I don't expect a reply and I won't be commenting on any other hateful e-mails. Enjoy your vacation! - Cher

**E-mail from Nate to Cher, dated 6/13/2008**

You most certainly did say some bad things about me. I read it in the e-mail you sent to Janet. There was nothing that I was going to say that wasn't going to get twisted by you, your mother, or know-it-all sister.

As far as white trash, look at yourself and your family. Have a nice life living off the taxpayers.

I did not reply. I cut all ties here and with Dante, who had not stayed clean.

## Ten

# Planes, Train wrecks and Denial

I had lost about eighty pounds in the year since Travis died. At first it was just not eating much because I was grieving, but then it turned to, "Hey, I think I can do this." People would ask me how I did it. Here's my answer. I stopped eating shit. After those first eighty pounds, I added walking at night for thirty minutes. Diet and exercise. Duh.

Angela started receiving e-mails that simply read: "Bipolar Bitch." Someone got into my e-mails (my password was "Amaya"...not hard to crack), and was not only reading my e-mails, but then was sending them to Agnes. They were private e-mails to Sue and others in which I often vented about my mom.

Someone contacted Social Security and tried to report me for working. You can work a limited number of hours while on Social Security. I was doing nothing wrong. Someone called the IRS to report the health care agency. They were audited and owed over $10,000.00.

All of this happened within a few months. The e-mail to my sister was from an e-mail address that had "torchy" in it. After some research, Mom found out that "torchy" was a World War II plane. Nate loved planes. Shit, he owned a plane!

I'm certain he e-mailed my sister, contacted Social Security, and called the IRS. I mean, who else could it have been? I very much expected Child Protective Services to show up at my door one day. *Let me guess, Nate sent you? Come on in.* Still, I don't regret reaching out to Nate despite Travis' warning. He should know his son died. I will *always* feel it was the right thing to do.

**A gift with a price**

"Lorenzo and I want to buy condos for you and your sister. You'll pay rent every month and when the condo is paid for, you'll own it, not us," Mom smiled.

I was overwhelmed. What a gift. I found the perfect two-bedroom, two-bathroom downstairs condo in a small development in the Lakes area. It had one owner, a little old lady who was also a widow. The carpet was purple, but I saw past that and added into my budget to have beautiful wood floors installed instead. The glass shower doors in the master bathroom had a "C" etched in them. See, I told you it was perfect.

Lorenzo got a letter from the homeowners association for Angela's condo, so one day while Angela was at work, he drove over there. She was stealing power from her neighbor. He followed the orange extension cord up her stairs into her living room to a small lamp next to a pillow and blanket. Every room was trashed, every room filled with drug paraphernalia, every room covered in smoke residue, tin foil pieces, and empty balloons. The toilet had obviously been clogged for months, but was still being used. Travis' TV? Only the impression it had left on the carpet remained. Angela was done pretending. Pretending to care about her job, pretending to be clean and sober.

I made the regrettable mistake of taking Amaya to Angela's condo to help Mom clean it. It didn't take long for her to just start sobbing. Amaya calls my sister EE. She couldn't say Aunt Angela when she was little, but she got out the sounds EE and it just stuck. She also calls Luke, Luke-a. Tommy is just Uncle Tommy as he was basically a stranger to her. Whenever I would ask him if he could babysit or take her out for ice cream, there was always an excuse. Tommy even forgot his only niece's seventh birthday. Boy, was I pissed off about that one.

Angela's drug use was hard on all of us, especially Amaya. As an adult, it is hard to not take the actions of a drug addict personally. For a child, it is that much harder. Since Amaya was six years old, she had been watching Angela struggle. The first time I put Amaya in counseling was at age six to deal with Travis' death. The second time, she was ten. This time, Amaya asked to go. It was after my sister had gone missing.

"Kids are resilient. She'll be fine," Amaya's therapist told me in 2007 and again in 2010.

Lorenzo was done with my sister after she had stolen his car to go buy drugs, and Agnes followed his lead. Sam was now living in Arizona, and Angela was sent to live there. She got off the bus in Phoenix and immediately scored drugs there.

## Love and Marriage

"Mom, I think you should go on a date," Amaya suggested.

It had been a few years since Travis passed away. I took that time to heal my little family. Amaya and I have always been close, but Travis' death had made us that much closer. Amaya slept with me most nights too. It brought me as much comfort as it did her.

I continued losing weight, going from a size 24 to a 12. Men looked at me again but I had been telling the ones who were brave enough to approach me that I was gay. I didn't have to let anyone down this way. I hadn't dated since John and James back in high school really, and things moved quickly with Brett and me, and even quicker for Travis and me. I was ready and open to the idea of love again. I was just waiting for Amaya to be ready.

Tommy was getting married. Not to Autumn, his fiancé since high school, who was there during my abortion. Mom and Autumn remain super close. Angela and I like to say Autumn is the daughter Agnes never had...

Not to fiancé number two, a psycho girl named Beth whom, when at Agnes' house, would turn photos of Autumn face down.

Not to Tammi. A girlfriend he married in the summer of 2007 so she could get her green card. The family didn't know about that marriage until someone tipped Agnes off, and she verified it on the Clark County Marriage License Bureau's web site.

Not to Marie. The mother of the son Tommy denied until a paternity test proved otherwise. He then quickly terminated his parental rights. The family didn't know about Tommy's son until Tommy was served court papers (at Mom's house) for child support.

Tommy was marrying Krissy. A woman with a history of drug abuse. A woman who had been thrown in jail once for beating up my brother.

Facebook came into my life in 2009. I was able to reconnect with my large extended family that I hadn't seen really since I left New York. Where had Facebook been my whole life? Catherine was also on Facebook, and that's how we reconnected too.

Tommy had a huge gambling, drinking, and pill problem by this point. Catherine and his dad, Thomas, bailed him out of several debts. Problem was that Tommy was also getting money for the same debts from Mom and Lorenzo. I did e-mail Catherine about what happened when I was sixteen, but she did not respond to it so I let it go. Sometimes you have to learn to accept the apology you never got.

"I am concerned Tommy is back to his old ways," I expressed to Catherine.

"You know, Cher, we are starting to realize Tommy wasn't the golden child we thought he was. I also don't know how they could be paying for this lavish wedding on their salaries," Catherine added. Being told that was enough of an apology for me.

Thank God for Sam. Did I just type that? After Mom washed her hands of my sister, it was Sam who was there for her. Sam made mistakes as a young stepdad to me. He'll admit that. I was a bratty teenager who really didn't give him a chance. I'll admit that. Once he no longer held the title of my stepdad, we were cool. I'll forever be thankful that he took my sister in and did whatever he had to do for her.

Sam didn't have the money to send Angela to rehab like Agnes and Lorenzo did, but he made sure she got on Methadone and to see her counselor. Angela had periods of sobriety in Arizona. But Sam also forgave her every time she relapsed and he would come home to find out that his stereo or golf clubs had been pawned. He never gave up on her. That's what a parent is supposed to do—never give up.

I had been on a few dates with a professional gambler, a waiter, a lawyer, and a disabled teacher. The teacher left cookies he baked for me at my door after I broke it off with him. Hello, Stalker! None of them were worthy enough to meet Amaya. I worked with family, volunteered mostly with women at Make-A-Wish®, and had never been much for the bar scene. I met these men on an online dating site.

I was starting to think I'd be single forever. If what I was dating was the best of what was out there, I was fine with that. I had plans to delete my profile when I got a message from some guy named Gregg. I thanked him for the message, mentioned I wasn't looking to date right now, and that I was meaning to delete my account. I wish I could tell you what he wrote back because it was funny and I'm a sucker for funny.

We sent a few messages back and fourth. He was genuine and sweet so I gave him my phone number. I hadn't spent hours on the phone like that since high school. I opened up to him about Travis. I wanted to be upfront that I was a widow and had a child. It was eerie what we had in common.

I worked for my family. He worked for his family. I had several stepdads. He had a few stepdads and stepmoms. Like me, he wasn't always treated well by them either. I lost a spouse to addiction. He lost a sister to addiction. One of the slimeball pain management doctors Travis used, Kimberly, his sister, was also involved with. As big as Las Vegas is, we lived just blocks from each other. We both loved blue M&M's and the movie *Se7en. "What's in the box?"*

Our first date was set. Chicago Brewing Company on Ft. Apache. He was sitting on a bench in front of the restaurant when I pulled up. *Thank God he looks like his profile picture,* I thought. He was a dead ringer for Seth Rogen at the time. We also both liked dark beer. "I bet I can down mine faster," I challenged. He won. I had an escape plan in place too. Angela would call me a half an hour in and I'd fake an emergency if I wanted to leave. I didn't need it.

Gregg was disappointed I could only stay for dinner so I knew he liked me. I had left Amaya home for the first time by herself. I was only five minutes away, but I was anxious to get home, even if I was just gone an hour. He called me later that night and I appreciated that. No games. How refreshing.

For our second date I remember buying shorts that were the smallest size I had worn since high school. I couldn't believe it! We met at an oyster bar. I don't like oysters. If we had been dating a year, I would have wanted to go somewhere else but we were still obviously in that "I'm cool with everything" stage. We also saw the movie, *Dinner with Schmucks.*

After date two, I told him I had MS. I did my best to explain what it was, and I advised him that if he looked online, to remember that everyone with the disease has different symptoms. He really didn't seem fazed. He was so unfazed that it was actually disconcerting to me.

Date three was at Gregg's house. I walked in, and *Friends* was on TV. I had told him in passing that it was my favorite show of all time (I'm 50% Monica and 50% Phoebe). He also made me a nice steak dinner at my request. I liked this guy. When I had briefly dated the waiter, he told me that he expected sex by date three, but because I was a widow new to the dating scene again, he'd give me a pass for a while. Geez. Thanks!

You can see why I thought I'd be single forever. After the steak dinner date, I took Gregg out to dinner and I paid. I think that's fair. I'm not expecting any guy to pay for me all the time. Gregg was very uncomfortable with me paying, but I told him to get over it.

Around date five we did have sex. I was ready because in part I knew Gregg wouldn't hurt me emotionally. I was nervous because I hadn't been with anyone since Travis died. In three years! I had nothing to worry about. Remember my best friend, Julia? The one I couldn't go to the NKOTB concert with? I called her the next day, gushing about my wonderful passionate night. We had the kind of sex that you high-five each other about afterwards.

Gregg was delightfully different, so it was time for him to meet Amaya. We met at a Chuck E. Cheese, as it was a great place to see how Gregg interacted with her. He passed with flying colors. As Gregg and I went our separate ways that night, I nervously looked at Amaya through the rearview mirror and asked, "So, what did you think?"

"He's really pale, like a ghost," Amaya was quick to reply.

Even before Travis died, it was just Amaya and I. While Travis worked, I stayed home most of her young life, or just worked part-time. We were together every day and our worlds revolved around each other. Amaya was fine with me dating in theory, and she didn't mind the few guys before Gregg as those never turned into anything more than a few dates. But now Gregg was a threat. Amaya wrote this letter a few weeks after meeting him and he started coming over often. She slipped it under my door one evening.

Dear Mom,

I am sorry but I feel uncomfortable with you dating. I feel like our relationship has crumbled. I cant live here if you date Gregg. I am not ready for you to start dating. Please dont do this.

If you sit down and talk to me I might understand. My life has been ruined, and broke into pieces. I don't know anyone to call but my friends because I know *Ama will say no (to me moving there). Can we work this out?

It is true I feel like I can't call you mom, our relationship has crumbled. I would feel better if you dated when I was ten and a half. I can't even cry anymore. My eyes are dried up. Please read this and talk to me. - Amaya

* Ama is the name my mom gave herself because she didn't want to be called grandma.

I took Amaya's "pain" seriously. Was our relationship crumbling? Of course not, but I wanted to validate and address her concerns. What I wouldn't have given back in the day for Agnes to do the same for me when it came to Sam.

"I read your letter and I want to talk about it. Can I ask you a question?" I asked Amaya.

"Yes."

"What does Gregg do that you don't like?"

Amaya thought about this for a few seconds.

"Nothing," she answered softly.

"Okay. If he's a nice person, and Mommy is happy, isn't that good?" I always spoke to Amaya like an adult (age appropriate). She was easy to reason with. She knew she had no reason to dislike Gregg. I reassured her that Travis would always be her father and that she came first, no matter what.

Tommy got married that fall. Catherine and Thomas were there and it wasn't awkward to see them this time because I was talking to Catherine often online and on the phone. When Tommy graduated college in 2000, I was pregnant with Amaya and saw them at his graduation. That time WAS awkward and we hardly spoke.

They later sent me a gift when Amaya was born, which was kind. Mom showed no interest in throwing me a shower, so Travis and I bought all of Amaya's baby clothes with a store credit card we never planned on paying back. Everything else we bought one item at a time when we could. Agnes did buy Amaya's crib, and once Amaya outgrew it, I passed it onto my dear friend from the heater company, Ro, for his son.

The wedding was beautiful on the clearest and nicest of October days in 2010. We stood overlooking Lake Las Vegas as Tommy and Krissy exchanged vows. My beloved brother Luke walked me down the aisle as I took my place next to my sister, Angela. She had a few months clean at the time.

I had been dating Gregg a few months, but Tommy said I couldn't bring him due to cost. I knew this was bullshit. Still, I didn't push the issue. I didn't know it at the time but this day would be the last day Amaya, Angela, Luke, Tommy, Lorenzo, Agnes, and I would all be together in the same room.

# Eleven

# Love And Hate

**E-mail to Gregg, sent by Cher on 11/3/2010**

Hi,

We will discuss this in person (if u still want to take me out Sat…) but sometimes it's easier for me to write down what I want to say.

I'm telling you this b/c I want too, not b/c I expect anything said in return. Maybe it's my (Make-A-Wish®) wish child dying but his passing does remind me yet again that life is short.

I know you're at least falling in love with me, whether you admit that to me or not. Like you've said, I can tell by the little things you have said/done over the last three months. I haven't said those three little words to anyone in years and frankly, I never thought I would again.

I've been pretty guarded w/the guys I've dated b4 u so this isn't easy for me, but I don't care.

I love the way u make love to me. Love that u make me laugh. I love the way u approach the situation w/Amaya. I love that you wanted to go to Chuck E. Cheese (again) and let Amaya win when u hate to lose. I love that u cooked for me. I love that you buy me gifts for no reason. I love that u know I love *Friends*, and had it on when I came over for our third date. I love that u sat through *Glee* even if only b/c you knew u would get some after. I love that you take me shooting b/c u worry about our safety. I love that u call me every day. I love that u check on me when I'm sick or I'm having a bad day.

I LOVE U. Yeah, damn, I said it first. What?! Well I typed it first…just don't write bk "thank you"…- Me

I lied. I did want him to say it back. When he said he'd stop by later to discuss my declaration of love, I fully expected Gregg to say it back. He did not.

"I haven't said those words to anyone in a very long time," he said.

"Well, me either," I interrupted.

"I haven't said it since I was a teenager." I knew his story. Gregg had a steady girlfriend in high school that he loved but she cheated on him. After his sister died, he went into a depression, only leaving the house to go to work. He lost interest in most social interaction. Years later, he pulled himself out of it, started dating, and I was only the second girl he went out with. I decided to give him a break.

"Okay, well you don't have to say it back. I feel this way and I want you to know it." Less than a week later, Gregg told me he loved me. He would later admit that he did love me when I expressed my love for him. He was just too afraid to say it back.

Months later, I told Amaya first. Then I called Gregg, he was dead asleep.

"I have to tell you something."

"Huh?" he murmured softly.

"I'm pregnant."

"Sounds like fun," he replied.

I know I woke him up with news you don't want to hear from your girlfriend of five months, but "sounds like fun?" I told him to call me back later. He called back pretty quickly, fully awake.

"I'm sorry, I just wasn't expecting that news from you. Let me take you and Amaya out to dinner later and we'll talk."

Any remaining resentment Amaya secretly carried for Gregg just left that day.

Gregg and I had actually broken up very briefly a month or so into our relationship over the issue of having children. After Travis died, I thought I was done. My health was holding up, but I couldn't imagine having any more children with anyone else. Gregg is six years younger than me. We met when I was thirty-five and he was twenty-nine. He envisioned kids in his future. I certainly did not. It was Agnes who gave me some sound advice. "If the worst thing about this man is that he wants to maybe have kids with you one day, be open to it."

She was absolutely right. Yet I had Amaya tell my mom that I was pregnant. She seemed happy enough. My brothers were concerned because Gregg and I hadn't been dating long, which was fair but Mom assured them I knew what I was doing. Lorenzo was hard to read. Everyone liked Lorenzo, and Lorenzo liked everyone. However, Lorenzo was cold toward Gregg for some reason.

I had met Gregg's mom a month or so after we started dating as she happened to be in town visiting from CA. Gregg loved his grandparents, and we never went out Friday nights because that's when he took them to dinner. Adoring your grandparents! Something else we had in common. I fell in love with his grandparents too. I met his dad and stepmom once I found out I was pregnant. Guess they figured they should get to know Amaya and me at that point.

"You and Amaya should move in with me," Gregg announced.

"What about my condo?"

I talked to Mom and Lorenzo and we agreed that I would rent it out. In late March of 2011, when I was almost three months pregnant, Amaya and I moved up the street into Gregg's home. That was the logical thing to do, I know, but it didn't feel like home to me. I was hormonal and worried. What was I doing? Did I really want to be here? Weren't we moving too fast? Amaya was so excited though, so I kept my doubts to myself.

Gregg had bought a 2011 Toyota RAV4 when he heard I was pregnant because he thought we should have a family car. He also bought me and Amaya little gifts all the time. Once we moved in he had told me, "You don't really need to tell me about your daily purchases."

I wasn't used to this. On my own, at times, I had to rob Peter to pay Paul as the saying goes. I got us to Disneyland every year and Ohio to visit Sue and Gordie every other year. Then some weekends, I had only a few bucks to my name. Amaya and I would pass the time by playing board games, going to the library, and watching movies at home. We also loved going to Sunset Park and then watch the airplanes land at McCarran.

Angela had relapsed again. She was living on the streets in Arizona and we didn't know where she was. Gregg had a soft spot for my sister, having lost his own sister to addiction. I was also eating for two again. This time though, it was more like eating for four. Soon I quickly was over two hundred pounds again.

When an ultrasound revealed we were having a son, we desperately searched for a name, even turning to our DVD collection for inspiration. "What about Cameron from *Ferris Bueller's Day Off*?" Amaya asked. Cameron. We all liked it!

Cameron Michael Finver would be here in just four and a half months. We had celebrated Mother's Day 2011 at my mom's house. I came home and noticed a little blood on my underwear. When it continued into Monday, I called my OBGYN, Dr. C. He had delivered Amaya, and he'd be delivering Cameron.

I knew spotting wasn't that uncommon, at least not in the first trimester. I was in my second trimester, but I really wasn't that concerned as I drove to Dr. C.'s office. He was at lunch but his staff was waiting for me to do an ultrasound. The sonographer was very reassuring.

"Sometimes our equipment can't pick up the heartbeat. The doctor will be back in thirty minutes. He'll find it." I left, and hit a nearby McDonald's, scarfing down my food as I waited for Dr. C.

He couldn't find Cameron's heartbeat either. "Dr. C. wants to send you to the high-risk pregnancy center a few buildings down. Their equipment is more high tech."

I called Gregg. He'd meet me there and I asked Mom to pick up Amaya from school. I don't know if it was denial or if I really thought Dr. C. had outdated equipment. I walked into the high-risk center with high hopes that were quickly destroyed. This sonographer was cold, not even giving a second thought to the damage her words would do.

"This baby has no heartbeat." I covered my mouth to stifle my screams. She left the room to get a doctor as Gregg walked in.

"There's no heartbeat," I cried out. Gregg sat silently beside me, trying to comfort me. I called Mom, asking her to tell Amaya. I couldn't bear to do it. We were told to go back to Dr. C.'s office. When we walked in, Tommy and Krissy were there. They lived close by and Mom must have called them. Tommy had his faults, but when I really needed him, he seemed to just show up.

The tech, who had been so reassuring an hour earlier, was gently discussing our options with us.

"You can go to the hospital and deliver him. Or you can go to sleep and have him removed."

"Which would you do?" I sobbed.

"Honestly, and Dr. C. won't discuss this with you for religious reasons, I'd go to sleep and have it be over."

I didn't want to go through delivery with Gregg at my side, and hear only silence as our son was born. Those were memories I never wanted to have. I chose to go to sleep. I detest the month of May. Travis was born in May. Eight days later, he died in May. Now, I was told Cameron had no heartbeat in May. He was removed from my womb the next day.

"You can't bring your daughter in here. It could upset some of our other patients," the receptionist instructed. She refused to buzz us in with Amaya there.

"I'll take her to lunch, then the mall," Mom offered.

"No, I want to stay with my mom," Amaya argued, she then reluctantly conceded.

There were no protesters outside of the abortion clinic that day. Good. I wasn't in the mood. I wasn't there for an abortion. I wanted this baby. I didn't want to be here. This was so unfair. I vented all of this to the counselor I was forced to see before the procedure.

"Just so you know, most of our clients are here for the same reason." I never knew that about these clinics. How awful that any woman who wants a baby, but loses it, has to make a choice between a funeral birth or this. Gregg waited for me in the lobby as I drifted into unconsciousness.

Before his passing, we had started to buy bedding and such for Cameron's room, which was going to have a *Lion King* theme. I couldn't bear the thought of having to face the sales clerk, so I asked Mom, and she returned it all for me. Gregg, Amaya, and I spent the next few days home together. We'd talk, cry, and play card games, trying to heal. Amaya had a question that I could not answer at the time. "Why did this happen?"

In our garage, Gregg and I coped by smoking weed, a lot of weed. I'd break down and start sobbing between tokes.

"You need to know something, Cher. If we never have a child together, you and Amaya are enough."

Gregg was so very loving during this time and he took such great care of me. It was in those days that I knew, when I did have my next MS relapse, he'd be able to handle it. And I was right.

I wanted to try again. I had decided pretty quickly that was the only way to make this pain go away. Gregg is a worrier. "Let's see what the doctors say," he'd say. I also wanted to know why. Why did Cameron die? Blood test results showed I have a blood clotting condition called Factor V Leiden Mutation. What most likely happened is that I developed a clot, and Cameron could not get the nutrients he needed. I called Gregg, collapsing on the floor.

"I killed our baby. It's because of me," I cried.

We could have tried again if I wanted to subject myself to daily shots of blood thinners in the stomach for my entire pregnancy and post delivery. I didn't think I could do that. Gregg didn't want me to do that. Gregg and my neurologist, Dr. T., were worried another pregnancy could be too stressful on my body. The decision was made for me. We would not try again. When I asked how come there were no issues like this during my pregnancy with Amaya, I was told the same answer by several of my doctors, "She is a miracle."

Amaya was tested a few years later. She has the same blood clotting condition. Precautions you can take are: living a healthy lifestyle, drinking lots of water, exercising, no smoking, and no birth control with certain hormones in it. Shit, I was, at one time, almost three hundred pounds, a smoker for over ten years (except when pregnant), and on and off birth control since the age of seventeen. How I didn't develop a blood clot sooner is beyond me.

After Cameron passed, Gregg gifted me his RAV4. Shortly after that, we moved into a house in a luxury, guard-gated, golf course community called Rhodes Ranch. Mom and Lorenzo were not happy about the car or our house for some reason. "We looked in Rhodes Ranch too," Mom made sure she noted, and not in an, "Oh, what a coincidence" way, but in a, "We could afford to live there too, you know" kind of way. When I told this to a friend, it was the first time someone had mentioned to me that my mother could be jealous of me. I couldn't wrap my head around this. Don't we all want our kids to do better in life than we did?

Being friends with my mother on Facebook was getting annoying too. She'd comment something sweet and supporting on a family member's status, yet she'd talk shit about them to me at the office. I really felt she crossed a line when she wrote on Facebook that she hated living in Las Vegas. That's not the part that really upset me. In the comments of that thread, she commented that the only reason she stays in Las Vegas is because of her friends at the SunCoast (her favorite casino). *Um, three of your four children live here, as well as your granddaughter...*

I guess that annoyance went both ways because Agnes had unfriended me on Facebook once. Unfriended by my own mother on Facebook. Who else can say that? Anyone? This was before I had a smart phone or a laptop. I went to Disneyland and came back to see that my notifications said we were Facebook friends again. I asked Agnes how that happened and she said she didn't know. But I know there is only one explanation.

When I was out of town with no access to my account, she went into my account (she set it up for me and knew my password) and refriended herself. Just tell me you're sorry for unfriending me in the first place. Don't play dumb. We all know Facebook can't refriend people on its own.

Lorenzo was having trouble sleeping and asked me for some pot. After asking if Mom was okay with it, I had Gregg get some. I left a message for Lorenzo that I would be stopping by soon. That's when Mom texted me.

Agnes: What makes you think I am okay with you bringing drugs into my home with Luke here? We don't do drugs.

Bullshit. When Mom and Lorenzo first starting living together, Angela went into their room looking for a sewing kit and called me crying after she found some weed in their closet. Years later, Sam told my sister that when he first got together with Agnes, they SOLD COCAINE. But I'm in the wrong trying to help my stepdad sleep?

Gregg asked me to marry him exactly one year from our first date. We went back, this time with Amaya, to Chicago Brewing Company and under the same sad little tree he stole a first kiss from me, he kneeled down. "Will you marry me?" Of course, I said yes. He is my happily ever after. Even if he thinks Star Trek is better than Star Wars, which it is not.

Do you know that one year for Christmas, Gregg gifted me with Donny and Marie Osmond dolls? They were just like the ones Agnes would take away from me when I was younger. As you know, I'm named after Cher. Well, Gregg was named after Gregg Allman of the Allman Brothers Band. Cher and Gregg Allman were married in the 70's, so anytime I go to Best Buy, I put a Cher CD next to a Gregg Allman CD just because.

"If you don't have an unlimited bar at your wedding, no one in our family will come," Mom sneered.

That was one of the last straws. I was getting tired. Tired of my mom being a functioning, embarrassing, alcoholic mess. Tired of not being appreciated at work. Tired of them not treating Gregg with the respect he deserved. Tired of Mom only spending time with Amaya by taking her shopping every few months. Tired of her fake Facebook ass. Tired of the way she treated my sister, and handled her addiction all these years. Tired of the way she coddled my brothers. Just tired.

Krissy's mother had died before her wedding to my brother. Agnes and Lorenzo had plans to go to their condo during this time, the condo they own and could go to anytime. They wouldn't reschedule, so it was just Amaya and I representing our family at the funeral.

I had this in mind when I told Gregg that we should just get married when Agnes and Lorenzo again had plans to be at their condo. Luke was also going with them on that next trip out of the country. It worked as Mom once again refused to reschedule. Good. I didn't want Mom and Lorenzo there anyway.

Tommy walked me down the aisle. Amaya was, of course, my maid of honor. Krissy was there as well as one of Gregg's friends and his girlfriend. Sue, Gordie, Gregg's mom, and stepdad watched from the live online stream at Cupid's Wedding Chapel here in Las Vegas on 9/8/2011.

After age two, I never had the same last name as my mom. I didn't want to do that to Amaya.

"I can make it Cherilynn Dawn Johnson-Finver," I told her.

"Mom, that's a lot to write. Cher Finver is fine."

I at least wanted to ask her. I would have been Johnson-Finver if Amaya needed me to be. Once we were married, we made it Facebook official, and the response from friends and family was overwhelming. Agnes came back from her condo knowing we had gotten married. Remember she chose not to reschedule going to the condo they own. I must have felt guilty because I put together a wedding album of our best pictures for her. I showed it to Lorenzo.

"Very nice," he replied uninterested.

I handed it to my mother.

"I saw pictures. On Facebook," she said coldly.

"Well, this is all of them in an album for you."

"I don't want to look at it now. It's painful because I wanted to be there," she overdramatized.

*But Mom, there was no open bar.* She could have been there. She chose to go to her condo. She only cared that she looked like an ass for not being there to our friends and family. I had had it. I went to work that weekend, cleaned out my desk, took that wedding album back, and called Lorenzo.

"Lorenzo, I can't do this anymore. You know how Mom is. I quit."

He knew how Mom was. He was afraid of her for some reason like most people were. I also told him I had more than paid the depreciated value on my condo and that I would no longer be responsible for it. Hell, I sure did a better job with my condo than my sister had with hers. That's when the text messages from Agnes started.

Agnes: You're a bad mom.

Agnes: I hope Amaya turns out to be nothing like you.

Agnes: You're selfish.

Agnes: You're pathetic.

After six years, I stopped volunteering for Make-A-Wish®. After Cameron died, I needed a break from the emotional toll such a volunteer position called for. I started sorting donations at the Shade Tree shelter once a week instead. Yes, the same shelter I thought I was too good to stay at just a few years prior. We got settled into our new home, and I focused on the friends and family that were there for me during this time. This did not include my sister at the time or my brothers. My sister because she was still battling addiction. My brothers because they chose sides.

Tommy and Luke were now both working for Agnes and Lorenzo (Krissy too). Their jobs were tied up with Agnes, their cars, housing too. Sound familiar? This was the same boat Angela and I were once in. Listen to me when I tell you, that all comes with an unbroken sense of loyalty. Of course my brothers are their own people but you don't bite the hand that feeds you.

## Twelve

# Express Yourself (hey, hey, hey, hey)

I was on a Madonna high. This is my defense and my excuse. Meaning, I was about to see her in concert that night for the fourth time ever in 2012. I'm just in a better mood those days, and any day I'm going to Disneyland. Her music makes me want to dance, and we should all dance more. Way back in 1985, Agnes walked into my room, looked at all the Madonna posters that hung on my walls, and said, "In twenty years, no one will even know who she was." HA! This still cracks me up.

Mom and I had only been in touch a few times over the past year, via text, only when it related to my sister. She texted me the day of the concert about my sister, and I replied. That led to the following e-mails.

**E-mail sent by Cher to Agnes on 10/15/2012**

Mom,

I asked Amaya yesterday if she wanted to see you, Luke-a, and Tommy and she shook her head yes. There were times she shook her head no. I even had her in counseling (again) earlier this year about it, but if she's ready, maybe I can try to be ready too.

I believe everything happens for a reason. (Angela's friend dying and you texting me about it. Angela again struggling, and us putting our shit aside to keep each other updated on her.)

I can try to forgive you for calling me a bad mom. Even though I know this is not true, it hurt a lot. I don't know why.

I still feel you drink and gamble too much. I want to try but I don't know how to do this, and still have a relationship with you.

If I said other things that hurt you, I am sorry.

After Travis died (I'll never deny how much you and Lorenzo helped me then), we just really didn't talk about the issues that led to us not talking for a year prior to his death. I don't think that was healthy and I don't want to make the same mistake again.

I don't think we'll ever have the same relationship we once did (at least I can't imagine it at the moment) but maybe for the sake of our family, we have to try. I just don't know how. - Cher

**E-mail sent by Agnes to Cher on 10/17/2012**

Cher,

I also believe everything happens for a reason.

That being said, let me reply as honestly as I can.

I called you a bad mother because I couldn't understand why you wouldn't encourage Amaya to see or at least stay in touch with me. I have only loved that girl and thought you'd understand that. I know Amaya has a mind of her own but she is still a child, and I guess I expected you to put aside our differences this time. Again, I'm trying to be honest. I know you adore her and, no, you are not a bad mom as I've told you many times. I was just hurt but am truly sorry for having said that.

Also, regarding the picture album…That hurt more than I can express. The fact that you didn't want me there, then turn around and give me pictures as to rub it in. Please understand how I felt.

Your judgment about what you think I do too much is your opinion. I'm not going to try to defend myself other than to say maybe you need to spend a night out with us. You probably would out drink and out play me. Doesn't matter though, I am almost 59 years old, owe no one, and do what I'd like. As can you.

I too think we need to talk over old baggage and try to clear the air. These e-mails are a good start. I can't wait for the time when we've gotten to the point of reestablishing our relationship. I positively think it can be done.

I DO love you Cher. But I think that in your heart you know that. Love, Mom

**E-mail sent by Cher to Agnes on 10/17/2012**

Hello,

I've always parented Amaya with the mindset that she can make her own decisions (on most things.) For a long time, she did not want to see you, so I didn't think I should force her. She has a lot of awesome female influences but you are her only living grandmother and she does love you/ is ready to see you now, and that is a big reason I'm trying here.

Regarding the photo album. I never thought about it in the perspective you wrote.

When Amaya and I were putting it together…I had a little guilt that you were not at the wedding (I'll get to that in a minute) so I wanted to at least put an album together for you. Please believe me when I say that I wasn't trying to rub anything in your face. I am so sorry you felt this way. Looking back, I now understand why you would feel this way.

I don't know if you remember this but in that short time Gregg and I were thinking about having a big wedding, you told me that no one in our family would come if we didn't have an open bar. This really stuck with me.

Gregg wanted to do what I wanted to do (as far as a wedding went) but told me he just wanted to be married. At the end of the day, that is all I wanted as well. His parents were not there either (and they all have a great relationship). Yes, I made it really hard for you to be at the wedding. I knew you were going to be at your condo.

I had a lot of frustration building about a bunch of things last September. I let things go/don't talk about them and then I just explode. I am working on not doing this. I bet last September that you didn't even think much was wrong, because I didn't discuss anything with you.

A few examples…Right or wrong…

The open bar comment.

I felt you and Lorenzo “checked out” of the business.

I felt I was under appreciated at work.

I hadn’t fully grieved Cameron’s passing, and I was angry and felt it was insensitive when you told me to just tie my tubes when we were trying to figure out what was next regarding trying again or which birth control method I’d have to use.

I didn’t understand why you didn’t seem happy for me that Gregg gave me the RAV4 or that we got a home. Looking back at that one, I guess you just wanted me to be careful/cautious. As a mom, I get that, but I also know that if Amaya does well or better than me in life so I won’t worry about her as much, I’d be overjoyed.

Yes, you can do as you like regarding the drinking and gambling. Know that my concern comes from a place of love. I worry. At the very least, we’ll agree to disagree.

Can I ask you a question regarding my brothers? I just really don’t understand their lack of contact. I was always a great sister to both of them. And Amaya doesn’t deserve this at all. I give Angela a lot of credit for staying neutral and loving us both.

```
I've heard rumors that Tommy/Krissy were
told or given the impression Krissy would
be fired if they talked to me. As far as
Luke, that one stings the most b/c well,
you know how we feel about him. There was
a period of time that Amaya couldn't even
talk about him without crying. - Cher
```

In regards to the open bar comment, Mom wrote back, "I know my family…they expect to party at a wedding." Know that we had planned on having wine and beer, but I guess that wasn't good enough for her. She denied holding Krissy's job over her head and that her sons are protective of her, picking "Team Agnes" as she put it. She admitted to checking out of the business (they were trying to sell it for awhile), and she apologized if I felt unappreciated because I did an excellent job.

Looking back though, when she refused to admit or acknowledge her drinking and gambling addictions yet again, I should not have gone any further with her. Although both she and Lorenzo have driven drunk I'm told, she never drove Amaya around while intoxicated, nor did she ever say she was taking Amaya shopping, ending up at a casino with her instead. Still, these were two of my main long-standing issues with her, and she blew them off, as addicts tend to do.

Mom and I ended up meeting at a Denny's after our e-mail exchange. I cried when we embraced. At the end of the day, we all need our mothers. Even me. We talked some more about the issues brought up in our e-mails, but the conversation turned to catching each other up on our lives over the last year. I wanted to see Luke, who was now nineteen. Mom wanted to see Amaya, so we made plans for another lunch date soon, at an Applebee's.

Mom told me that my brothers and Lorenzo were sick of our fighting. I get that. I was sick of it too. We had been going back and forth now for years. It was toxic and draining for all involved.

I should also mention that I looked a lot different from the last time Mom saw me. I spent a good six months in 2012 going to the gym every damn day. I did have a trainer for nine weeks. He showed me how to use the equipment at our gym, giving me the tools I needed to get into shape. I looked better than I ever had. I had energy, I was strong, and I felt beautiful.

When I saw Luke at Applebee's, I just hugged him and it was as if no time had passed. I tried to invite Tommy and Krissy over to our new home. No reply. Lorenzo also did not have any interest in seeing us.

This was the same for my sister. Lorenzo really was done with her the day she took his car back in 2010. He had no contact with her from that day forward. Adult or not, I would find it odd and uncomfortable if Gregg had nothing to do with Amaya. When you marry a woman with kids, those kids are now your kids. Tommy never called, texted, or saw Angela either once she was shipped off to Arizona. As the matriarch of the family, why wouldn't you try to bring unity to the family, not divide it?

I now can look back and realize Lorenzo and Agnes are toxically perfect for each other. He doesn't mind having his balls in her purse, and he's right there with her, drinking and gambling. He dropped my sister. He dropped me. He dropped Amaya, and, for no reason, he never liked Gregg.

I don't really suffer from anxiety but I would get extremely anxious whenever my mom came over to pick Amaya up after that. I felt our relationship was fake and forced more than ever. She still drank too much and gambled four to five nights a week. She still only came around to take Amaya shopping, then post about it. Nothing had changed.

Around this time, I had reached out to the *Dr. Phil* show in regards to my sister and I actually heard back. Sadly, Angela was not ready and it fell through. This was when I had written a eulogy for my sister. I knew I couldn't write it when the day actually came. I felt it was a matter of when that day came, not if.

Drugs lead to three places: jails, institutions, and death. Angela had already been to jail several times, and Mom had her institutionalized when she was a minor. I still carried so much anger at our mother about how she handled my sister. This anger was something I never brought up in any of those e-mails, but I should have.

I hope I never know what it is like to have a child addicted to drugs, but I know this: I will fight for that child and I will put them in a rehab. If Gregg wants nothing to do with that child and doesn't understand we are dealing with a disease here, Gregg can kick rocks. The beginning of the end, for good this time with Agnes came in January of 2013.

Amaya was having a hard time in middle school. She was being bullied. This I did know, but I thought it was being handled. She'd get in the car and I'd ask, "How was your day," and she'd say, "Fine." She was twelve; isn't that the answer you'd expect from a preteen?

"Mom, I need to talk to just you."

"Of course."

"Mom, I just tried to hurt myself. I took a belt and tried to cut off my air supply."

I didn't see a red mark. She was breathing and talking normally. "We need to bring Gregg into this conversation. Don't you agree?" She did, and she calmly told Gregg. Then I got out her insurance card and called the twenty-four hour nurse hotline.

"Hi. My daughter just told us she is not in distress, but she has taken a belt and was trying to hurt herself. Because she is able to stand here and talk to me, I wasn't sure if I should call 911."

"Ma'am, if your daughter is telling you she just tried to kill herself, please hang up with me and call 911."

I hung up and sat down next to Amaya on the couch. "You know what this mean, right? An ambulance will come here, ask you questions, and then probably separate us. We'll have to go to the hospital too, and you could be there for days." I had an idea, from all the times my sister tried to commit suicide when she was younger, what the process was.

"I understand," Amaya told me.

With that, I dialed 911. Six long hours later, a counselor from Symphony Healthcare showed up to the emergency room. We were very familiar with them as Amaya had been going to Symphony on and off for years. We were separated but I was assured that most kids went home with their mom and dad. Gregg and I sat in the waiting room as Amaya was assessed.

"Your daughter is severely suicidal. She needs to be admitted to a psychiatric hospital at once." The counselor's words echoed in my head as I tried to make sense of this. A mental hospital? Amaya was only twelve-years-old.

I tried calling Agnes several times that night. As Gregg and I left the behavioral health treatment center early the next morning, my phone finally rang. It was Agnes. "I'm sorry, I sleep with my ringer off." *If one of my daughters was out there homeless (at times) and battling drug addiction, I'd sleep with the phone in my hand.*

Amaya was hospitalized for six days. Gregg and I visited every night. They wanted to start her on Zoloft and I reluctantly agreed. She was discharged with instructions to follow up at Symphony Healthcare for outpatient care, which we did.

Upon her release, I asked the counselor, "Why didn't I see signs?"

"Because she didn't want to you see them," was the answer. She went to therapy every other week, and a girl's self esteem group every week for most of 2012, focusing on her mental health.

My mother did not see Amaya for over three months after she was discharged from the mental hospital. Whenever

I'd invite her to come see her, there was always an excuse. Lorenzo and my brothers didn't call, text, or send a card. You may be mad at me but what did Amaya ever do to deserve being cut off like that? Nothing. She was a child. You know who cared? My sister.

"Let me get to a safe place to call you," she'd tell me.

Angela had been through a lot of what Amaya was now going through, so I don't care if she called me high. It was more like just trying not to be dope sick at that point. Her advice to me was invaluable. As Amaya was dealing with her depression and anxiety at Symphony, she asked several people in her life to attend counseling with her, including Agnes, so I texted her.

Cher: Amaya is asking if you'll attend a therapy session with her. I've gone. Gregg has gone.

Agnes: I don't know. I'm too old and tired.

That was it. I was done. Agnes is the most immature "acts-half-her-age" senior citizen I know. She's not too old and tired. She didn't want someone with a degree telling her what I've told her for years. *My daughter, your only granddaughter, is reaching out to you in a healthy, positive way, and you are too old and tired?*

Tommy also tried talking to Agnes about her addictions once he admitted his own. She blew him off too of course. Tommy told Gregg and me once that Agnes would always play a slot machine facing the sports book (where Lorenzo was) so she could quickly switch from playing quarters to just nickels whenever Lorenzo was walking back toward her. Agnes denies this.

# Thirteen

# Finding Answers

I walked into the Pediatric Pain Clinic at UCLA as prepared as I could be. It had been eighteen months since Amaya first had burst into our room complaining of chest pains. This is not something you expect your twelve-year-old to complain about. She also wasn't sleeping well.

When I first met with the medical students that were assisting Dr. Z., I handed them a timeline with all my corresponding medical records and tests neatly organized in a white binder. They were highly impressed that I had gone through so much trouble. I thought it was odd that all the other parents seeking the next level of care for their children didn't have a white binder.

We first heard the word "costochondritis" when we took Amaya to the emergency room on 8/13/12 when she had chest pains. Costochondritis is an inflammation of the cartilage that connects a rib to the breastbone. Despite being in excruciating pain, she was simply given Tylenol with Codeine and told to follow up with her pediatrician. We were back in the emergency room the very next day as the pain intensified.

These sharp, shooting, chest pains came and went without notice. It's an awful feeling having your child doubled over in pain and you cannot help them. Pain so bad she was excused from physical education for the school year. When her pediatrician was out of options, Amaya was sent to a rheumatologist. No medications were helping and all blood work ordered came back normal. A heart specialist was then brought in to do an echocardiogram. Those results were also normal.

After a year, the chest pains started to become constant. Twenty-four hours a day, my daughter was in such pain she couldn't get off the couch. I'm thankful Amaya is so intelligent. With so much school missed because of the pain, she was still able to keep up. A pain management doctor was up next. I had mixed emotions about this. I was desperate to help Amaya, but pain management doctors still left a bad taste in my mouth from Travis. Plus, Amaya was already having trouble tolerating the medication she had already tried. Still, I made the appointment.

He didn't seem to be trying to get Amaya hooked on drugs. He did, however, order an X-ray of the chest and spine. Normal. Entire body bone scan. Results were normal. Injections of something called Ketorolec Tromethamine relieved the pain for a whole two hours.

CAT scan ordered. Results were normal. Yet more injections were done. She'd have relief for a week, and then nothing. Finally, the decision was made to send Amaya to UCLA.

By the time Dr. Z. walked in, the anticipation was such that I felt like I was finally meeting the *Wizard of Oz.*

A wizard who would solve this mystery, and give my daughter her life back.

"Is this even costochondritis?" I asked.

"No," said Dr. Z.

*So Amaya had been misdiagnosed for eighteen months?!*

"I've heard growing pains, is it that?" I inquired.

"No. I believe Amaya had a muscle spasm. This is a signaling problem. The body remembers pain so whether the muscle is currently spasming or not, her brain thinks it is. I recommend you do biofeedback (a process whereby electronic monitoring of a normally automatic bodily function is used to train someone to acquire voluntary control of that function) and physical therapy in the water. Come back in six months."

I feverishly wrote down what Dr. Z. said as fast as I could. I was also handed a welcome packet with an insert for her book, *Conquering Your Child's Chronic Pain*. We returned home where I made appointments to start biofeedback and water physical therapy. I also ordered Dr. Z's book. In reading it, I finally felt like someone got it. Here is just some of what I highlighted:

*Even though the acute injury has been healed, the child's pain-signaling apparatus has been "turned on," and something is stopping the signals from being "turned off," stopping the body from returning to normal.*

*Some parents of chronic pain are frustrated by the lack of a concrete label for their child's pain.*

*I also get patients who have undergone unnecessary surgical procedures or are prescribed potent drugs simply because their doctors have run out of ideas and feel pressure to do something to alleviate the child's suffering.*

*Though anxiety does not cause pain, it can worsen pain by increasing the volume of pain signals.*

*About 80% of the children who come to our pediatric pain clinic have an underlying anxiety disorder.*

*Because the memories of pain remains in the brain, the nervous system keeps the pain going.*

*Chronic pain can cause a child to lose sleep, and a lack of sleep can cause more pain.*

Every week Amaya did water physical therapy. Every week she did biofeedback. For three months. New pain meds too but nothing was working. I wasn't giving up. I went back to UCLA as determined as ever.

I interrogated Dr. Z., "Could Amaya have Complex Regional Pain Syndrome Type 1? Amaya is extremely bright, and was involved with gymnastics before her pain started. Your book says gymnasts are at a greater risk of CRPS-1 and children with CRPS-1 tend to be bright and high achieving." I told you I was determined. Determined to have a correct diagnosis. Determined to find answers.

CRPS-1 is a debilitating painful disorder of a part of the body. Pain can occur after a surgery but may occur without a prior event. The pain can be described as stabbing or a shooting pain, which is what Amaya described it as. The painful body part may be sensitive to light or touch, which Amaya also had. CRPS-1 is caused by an abnormal turn on in the sensory nervous system.

"If you need to put a label on it, then yes," Dr. Z. said.

"Your book also talks about alternative methods to cure chronic pain. Can we try acupuncture?" I asked. Can you tell yet I was a little obsessed with her book?

"Not yet. I want you to try a different medication and get a sleep study done." I barely graduated high school. What did I know? I listened and made another appointment in three months. We did the sleep study. Amaya ended up having two sleep studies actually. Mild sleep apnea if you look at her on the child's scale, no sleep apnea on the adult scale.

Pain continued, frustrations mounted, and hope started to diminish, but I didn't dare let Amaya know that. I e-mailed Dr. Z., telling her I had made Amaya an appointment for acupuncture. How could it hurt? Amaya first saw Dr. Kelley in August of 2014.

I had heard of acupuncture before. I knew it involved needles. That was about it, until Dr. Z.'s book. It states that acupuncturists believe an energy force flows through the body. You can't see this energy but if its flow is blocked or unbalanced, you can become sick.

I nervously waited as Amaya emerged from the treatment room. Dr. Z. instructed me not to ask Amaya on a daily basis what her pain level was, but I couldn't resist. "So?" I asked as we thanked Dr. Kelley, and made another appointment.

"Level 5." We had assigned levels to Amaya's pain. 0 no pain, 10 lots of pain. A 5? I hadn't heard a pain level that low since Amaya started on this journey. A 5 I could work with!

Second visit. "So?"

"Mom, I don't have any pain."

We celebrated with lunch at Red Lobster. Ten minutes into lunch, I asked her, "Are you still not in any pain?" I thought this was all too good to be true. We had been through her pediatrician, a rheumatologist, a children's heart specialist, a pain management specialist, two sleep studies, and one of the most trusted chronic pain specialist in the country at UCLA. Granted it was Dr. Z.'s book that mentioned acupuncture as a possible course of treatment, but acupuncture was really the answer? My daughter had been in chronic pain at a level 9 or 10 for almost TWO years, and *this* was the answer?

"Amaya's Qi was blocked." Dr. Kelley said matter-of-factly.

So what is "Qi"? In English, Qi is often translated to mean energy. This energy flows through the meridians in the body in a manner similar to the nervous system. The presence of Qi is important in the organs and bodily systems that require large amounts of energy. However, to the Chinese, Qi not only powers a function, but it is inseparable from function. So there is no function without Qi, and no Qi without function. When Qi flows smoothly throughout the meridians, every organ, and bodily system are in harmony, and there is health, but when Qi is blocked, there is pain and illness.

Amaya continued to be pain-free as our next trip to UCLA approached. I was thrilled to report this to Dr. Z. She asked for Dr. Kelley's contact info so she could refer other patients of hers here in Vegas. I would tell any parent to look into alternative medicine and methods of treatment sooner rather than later. I wish I had.

During these two agonizing years, Gregg was amazing. He was patient, understanding, and loving toward Amaya regarding her mental health and chest pain condition. Just think about the hospital stays, the countless doctor appointments, tests, and the cost to get to UCLA every three months. Would Thomas, Sam, or Lorenzo have been that patient, understanding, and loving if I needed all that as a child? This long chapter was closing for Amaya, and our little family, but there would be new challenges to overcome.

# Fourteen

# No Regrets

Back in 2013, I could barely get Tommy to return my calls. Then he texted me to tell me that Krissy was pregnant. Later, while angry at me for telling him he should have spent some time with a cousin visiting from out of town, he confessed that he only told me about the pregnancy because Mom was dying to post about it on Facebook. Hear that sound? That was my heart breaking. Tommy's relationship with Thomas and Catherine had been disintegrating now for a few years. Of course Agnes got in the middle of it, telling Catherine to, "Go get a family of your own."

Thomas, Catherine, and myself were not present for the birth of Tommy's (second) son. Weeks later, Krissy included me in a group text that included a photo of their newborn. No apology, no "let's talk," just a picture. I was stunned and hurt. *You haven't spoken to me in how long, and this is how you extend an olive branch?*

Although I probably should have been in therapy my entire life, I went to talk to a therapist for the first time in 2014, the same lady who was doing Amaya's biofeedback. Of course we spoke about my concerns and fears about

Amaya, but over the course of a few visits, my family was a regular topic of discussion.

"I'd like you to do something before our next appointment. I want you to write letters to your mom, Tommy, and Luke and then read them to me," she instructed.

"And then?" I asked cautiously.

"And then you can either mail them or rip them up," she replied.

I wrote Mom an angry three-paragraph letter. That anxiety I felt when Mom would come over to our house? I felt that again as I was writing. I was tense. I felt sick. I did my assignment and wrote something, but I knew before I wrote one word that I had no intention of mailing hers. I knew it would do no good and that my mom had no desire to change, or admit any fault. I felt differently about my brothers.

*4/24/14*

*Dear Tommy,*

*I want to start by saying I miss you. I get sad when I think about our family and how broken it is. I've been in therapy awhile. Just to have the tools to better deal with some things, some people. It's been very helpful. With this said, I am supposed to write some letters. Out of the three, Luke's and yours are the only ones I have even considered mailing. I struggle because I don't think I should chase anyone. But, I also think I should fight for what I love, and I love you.*

*I want to apologize for texting you when our cousin was here, I should have left that alone even though he tried more than once to text you. I was just taken aback by the way you spoke to me via text then. And I was hurt when you texted me that I was only told Krissy was pregnant, because Agnes wanted to post it on Facebook.*

*We used to be so close. You were my first best friend. Most of the wonderful memories from my childhood have you right there next to me. I know you pulled away as we got older, and you got involved in some things you now regret. I don't know...I thought things were turning around. I could have had anyone walk me down the aisle but I chose you.*

*I'm not here to bash Agnes but I have to bring her up. I just can't have a relationship with her. I'll never deny the good she has done but I feel, at this point, the bad outweighs it. If you ever want to hear my side, I'll tell you. If you don't, that is fine too. There are no teams here. You can love us both. Many do. I'm sorry for all the times we were on good terms and then not. I feel things always went back to sour mainly because past issues were never really dealt with and being honest (with oneself) is important.*

*You were not a very good Uncle to Amaya. I know it's hard to compare the relationships between Amaya and EE and Luke-a but you know what I'm saying. You were always distant. Never wanted to spend time with her, etc. This hurt me. I put myself in your shoes...you were going through some stuff a child shouldn't be around. Was that it? And Amaya trying to kill herself on 1/5/13...nothing. Not a card, not a call, nothing. I just don't get that.*

*And hello, I'd be the best aunt ever. I am so happy for you that you have a healthy beautiful son but at no time did you think, "Maybe I should try to fix things with my sister?" Again, I don't get it. I'll be honest. I was crushed when I heard Krissy was in labor. And maybe she was trying to break the ice, but including me in that one group text with a newborn baby pic wasn't the best way to reach out.*

*You may not write back or call/text but I had to try. If I didn't send this, I'd always wonder if I should have.*

*There is a letter here for Luke-a. Can you please make sure it gets to him? I heard he moved out (yeah Luke!) but I don't have the address. Thank you.*

*4/24/14*

*Dear Luke-a,*

*Some of this is in the letter I wrote to Tommy, but it sincerely reflects both of you:*

*I want to start by saying I miss you. I get sad when I think about our family and how broken it is. I've been in therapy for a while. Just to have the tools to better deal with some things, some people. It's been very helpful. With this said, I am supposed to write some letters. Out of the three, yours and Tommy's are the only ones I have even considered mailing. I struggle because I don't think you should chase anyone. But, I also think I should fight for what I love, and I love you.*

*I'm not here to bash Agnes but I have to bring her up. I just can't have a relationship with her. I'll never deny the good she has done but I feel, at this point, the bad outweighs it. If you ever want to hear my side, I'll tell you. If you don't, that is fine too. There are no teams here. You can love us both. Many do. I'm sorry for all the times we were on good terms and then not. I feel things always went back to sour mainly because past issues were never really resolved and being honest (with oneself) is important.*

*Next to Amaya, I loved (still love) you the most. How many times have you stayed at my house? I helped raise you and for many, many, many years, you were the best uncle on the planet.*

*After we sat in that Applebee's with Agnes and Amaya, I tried to reach out to you, and invited you over for dinner at least two times. I don't think I ever even got a reply. And when Amaya tried to kill herself, you did nothing. Not a card, not a call, nothing. I just don't get it. (?)*

*Then Amaya calls you about that one outdoor concert. It wasn't about going to the concert, it was that Amaya missed you. I don't understand how you can go from being SO close to her to nothing. Fuck if Agnes and me are fighting. What does Amaya have to do with any of that? Nothing. You are an adult. You can stand up for yourself, and say and do what you what. At any time in the last year or so did you say to yourself, "I should try to reach out to my sister and niece?"*

*You may not write me back or call or text but I had to try. If I didn't send this, I'd always wonder if I should have. Bottom line is this. I can't apologize or defend anything you are mad at me over if you won't talk to me about it.*

*Lastly, I'd like to say I can't believe you are 21. OMG. Happy (belated) Birthday. I heard you moved out (woohoo) too, that's huge! Congrats.*

I apologized in these letters. I called my brothers out in these letters. I told them I loved them and missed them.

I said all I wanted to say. To date, I have not heard back from either Tommy or Luke in regards to my letters.

In 2014, Angela moved with Sam to New Mexico to help take care of Sam's ailing mother. With better state programs there, she was able to get on a Methadone program and stopped using heroin. She has been clean since June of 2014. She did it on her terms, in her own time, without the help of our mother, but with all the love and support of her father. I finally had my sister back, my funny, intelligent, beautiful, thoughtful sister. Heroin often wins. Not here. Not now. I know how thankful I am that I can say that. Angela is a full-time college student, currently enrolled in a departmental honors program.

Agnes visits her once or twice a year so she can show everyone that she has a relationship with at least one of her daughters. Angela has definitely had periods of no contact with our mother, but her journey with her is different than mine, and I support my sister no matter what. At the end of the day, if you can have a relationship with your parent(s), you should, but on a regular basis do they talk? No.

Meanwhile, I just kept sneaking one. Then another. Soon I had to make a secret trip to replace the Sam's Club twenty pack of full-size candy bars I had eaten for Halloween that year. I was ashamed that all that hard work and hours I had put in at the gym in 2012 were gone.

Up and down my weight yo-yoed. Eat well for a few weeks. Eat crap for a few weeks. Why couldn't I control this? Angela had drugs, my mom had alcohol, and I had food. I was finally ready and able to admit that. There's a crude saying, "I eat garbage because I am garbage," and that's how I felt inside. I didn't believe I deserved to be the pretty girl I once was.

Now, I know I just told you I should eat better but if I had to turn forty, I was going to do it eating a churro in my happy place. Speaking of churros, those were Travis' favorite Disneyland snack. Once they went on sale at the park, he stopped going on rides and waited in line for one. Since his death, any time we are at Disneyland, we sit down and have a churro to remember Travis. Even Gregg.

Gregg had booked me a five-day Disneyland trip of my dreams in January of 2015. A stay at the Disneyland Hotel, three day hopper passes, dining at all my favorite Disney restaurants, a rest day at the spa at the Grand California AND a behind-the-scenes tour, the "Walk in Walt's Footsteps" tour. This Disney nut was in heaven! Unfortunately, Walt's apartment was closed for maintenance.

My condolence prize? A tour instead of the Disneyland Dream Suite above the *Pirates of the Caribbean* ride. Oh, it was everything you'd imagine it to be, and more. It would have been the perfect week, but you are only as happy as your saddest child.

Makeup covered up the scars well. Wearing long sleeves and pants helped too. Amaya had been lying. Burning herself, cutting herself, and then there were more attempts to end her precious young life. And, as we were about to leave for California, this:

"Mom, you know how models stay skinny? By like throwing up and stuff? Well, I've done that."

My own eating issues instantly shamed me.

"We should cancel our trip, let me call Gregg, and then make you an appointment to talk to someone over at Symphony."

"No, don't cancel. I want to go. I'll be okay. I'll get help when we return, promise. I can control it," Amaya begged. I had no idea of the depth of her eating issues as we left for the place with some of the most decadent food on the planet as far as the eyes can see.

We were dining at the beautiful Carathy Circle restaurant in Disney's California Adventure Park. It is a replica of the Carathy Circle theatre where *Snow White and the Seven Dwarfs* premiered back in 1937. We did our best to keep an eye on Amaya. But this meal, I remember, she ate, then convinced me she just needed to go to the bathroom. She came back euphoric.

I lost my shit. I'm at the "happiest place on earth" for my birthday, and Amaya and I are standing there, yelling at each other.

"Thanks for the amazing birthday week, Amaya," I screamed sarcastically.

"It's not my fault!" she shouted. She was right.

Amaya stormed off in front of us heading back to our hotel. Gregg started to cry as the fighting continued. "I don't want to see you two fight," he sobbed. This stopped us in our tracks, Gregg crying. We each apologized. Gregg and I continued to watch Amaya the best we could as we finished out our last day at Disney. We drove the four hours home, dropped our luggage off, and headed straight to the hospital.

We knew the routine. Wait for Symphony to come to the hospital and do an assessment. "She's not in immediate danger," the counselor stated. "Have her go see her psychiatrist, Dr. Still, on Monday."

"Am I supposed to just continue trying to watch her in the meantime?"

"Yes." That was an exhausting task, but we had been doing it all week. What were a few more days? Monday morning at eight, we were at Dr. Still's office. His plan? Pretty much more of the same counseling and group therapy she had been getting back in 2013.

I was given a short list of eating disorder support groups here in town. One had a disconnected number and the other was getting ready to shut down. Dr. Still did give me the number of a therapist that specialized in eating disorders. I called her but Amaya was placed on a waiting list. Amaya's frustrations mounted. The watching her at home continued. Keep her busy.

"Amaya, let's clean out the cabinets in the kitchen."

"Okay," she replied with no enthusiasm.

We had a large pile of items I could donate piling up.

"Let me go move some of this stuff to my room," I told her.

"Okay."

I was gone for maybe thirty seconds.

"I'm sorry, Mom."

She was closing the refrigerator, putting away the bottle of water she had just used to wash down a handful of her Trazadone prescription. This time I dialed 911 first. As I got in my car to follow the ambulance back to the hospital, I saw her. She was white, her lips purple. As they closed the door, I heard her throwing up. Good.

"There are no beds at the behavioral hospital. We'll have to hold her here until one opens up," the ER nurse said.

"Mom! I want to go home. NOW." Her lips were still black from the activated charcoal given to help absorb the drugs she had ingested.

"Amaya, you just tried to overdose, I can't take you home." I came back the next morning. Amaya had had a bad night. She was screaming at me from the bed she was given in the emergency room hallway. "I hate you! I want to go home!"

"That's okay. I love you," I said.

She was transferred later that day back to the behavioral hospital. It had been almost exactly two years since her first stay here. Gregg and I visited every day, despite us both having the flu. We'd stay in bed all day, rolling out of bed just to visit, and then we'd crawl back in bed. I know I should have stayed home, and I know I probably infected others, but there was no way I wasn't going to visit my kid. She was released five days later with instructions to follow up with Dr. Still.

Days later, "Mom, I'm having racing thoughts again." Amaya said. Her face was expressionless, her eyes blank.

"Get in the car, let's try to go back to the behavioral hospital."

It was raining cats and dogs as I raced across town. I called the hospital from the car. "Hi, my daughter was released a week ago but we need to come back," I yelled through my Bluetooth. "There are no beds open right now ma'am," I was told.

I pulled over at the M Casino's parking garage to escape the rain and dialed Symphony Healthcare's number. It was after hours so I pressed 1 as if I was hospital personnel in need of an assessment. I just had to get a live person on the line.

"Hi, I'm hoping you are a parent. Please look up my daughter's file. Her name is Amaya Johnson," I paused so he could do so. "She's been coming to Symphony Healthcare on and off since 2007. She was just in the behavioral hospital again last week. She is having racing thoughts. I just called the hospital but there are no beds. Please tell me where I can bring her."

"I *am* a parent. Hold on." I breathed a sigh of relief.

"Okay, you are correct, no beds. I wanted to check since you were headed there anyway. Do you know where Winter Valley Treatment Center is?"

"I do actually." Angela was supposed to do outpatient there one time, but took off running across the street, losing Agnes in the process.

"Go there."

"Thank you, thank you, thank you," I said as I abruptly turned to go back in the direction from which I had just come. Five minutes later, my phone rang. "Hi, this is Symphony Healthcare again. Winter Valley is also full. Take your daughter to the mental hospital on Maryland Parkway." Gregg met us there. Once her intake was done, the paperwork was signed, and she was ushered away. We went home and waited until we could visit.

Amaya had a scheduled appointment with Dr. Still. I went alone. "Amaya's not here because she's at another mental hospital. I wanted to talk to you by myself anyway."

The tears were swelling up, Dr. Still saw I was struggling so he spoke, "If you want to stop this cycle of short-term mental health hospital stays followed by therapy here for the rest of Amaya's life, you have to do more."

Here I thought we were doing everything we could do for Amaya. He continued, "There's a place in California called Destinations to Recovery. I used to work with their psychiatrist. It's Amaya's best chance."

That's all I had to hear. I went home and called them. I was directed to fill out some paperwork online. With Gregg as my back up, it was time to tell Amaya at our next visit. I took her hand, "We love you. We want you to get better. Don't you want to get better?" Amaya was back at being mad at me for admitting her, so I continued. "Don't you want to stop this cycle of hospitals and always being in therapy? There's a place that can help you. In California."

It took a few minutes, but Amaya agreed to go upon her release from the hospital but there was another pressing problem at hand. "My roommate. We were able to throw up together." That was bad. "And her mom," Amaya motioned to a table across the room, "brought in heroin for my roommate." That was also bad. "Once visiting is done, I'll ask to speak to someone," I said.

"No, don't," begged Amaya, "My roommate is violent. She'll know I told." We hatched a plan. I'd tell the hospital that I had to have Amaya discharged early so we could leave for Destinations to Recovery. Then I'd report the roommate and her awful mother. Which is exactly what I did.

We drove up the long winding roads of the canyon until we reached Destinations to Recovery. We were welcomed by staff and given a brief tour. Amaya and I were then separated. She was sent to talk to her family therapist and I was dealing with more paperwork. We were reconnected briefly to say our goodbyes. This wasn't a five-day stay in a mental hospital across town. This was a beautiful residential treatment center in California, a good six hours away from home.

"Don't leave me here, Mom! I'll jump off this mountain!" she threatened. In that moment, I was calm. I had to be. There was no way I could let Amaya know that her insurance just denied her stay here.

"Please don't run off the mountain. I'd chase you and I'll probably fall. Give me a hug. I will see you in a week." A week! I've never gone days without seeing my daughter, let alone a week. I had to come back to meet with her treatment team in a few days, and I was promised a short visit then. I drove straight home, and I didn't cry. I couldn't if I wanted to get home to Gregg safely. I walked in the door, saw Amaya's little shoes in the entry way and fell to pieces.

"You didn't sign up for this," I cried into Gregg's chest.

"Yes I did. The day I married you." Gregg meant it.

"What about the money, how are we going to afford this? I couldn't take her home. She was threatening to jump off the mountain. She needs this."

"I know. I'll talk to my dad and uncle and we will figure it out."

We paid what we could upfront, and Gregg's family loaned us the rest. I will never be able to thank them enough for that. Never.

I counted down the days until I was meeting with Amaya's treatment team. They didn't disappoint.

"Hello, I'm Amaya's physiatrist."

"Hello, I'm Amaya's family therapist."

"Hello, I'm Amaya's individual therapist."

"Hello, I'm Amaya's nutritionist."

"Hello, I'm Amaya's teacher while she's here."

And the introductions went on and on. Music, art, equine, and surf therapy?! At home, the resources for Amaya were so limited. I was happily overwhelmed by the care she was now receiving. I knew this was where Amaya needed to be but a comment Angela made really drove that home.

"I'm not saying I would have made all the right decisions, but if Mom and Lorenzo had done for me what you and Gregg are now doing for Amaya, I know my life would have turned out different." Besides having issues with Agnes never considering in patient help for my sister, whenever it came time back in the day for Angela's therapist to meet Agnes, Agnes would change therapists. Eventually Angela would just tell her new therapist, "If you want to keep me as a client, don't ask my mother to come in here."

I had been to therapy with Amaya numerous times. At Destinations, I knew this was different.

"We'd like you to attend Al-Anon," they told me.

"Sure."

"We'd like you to also be in therapy."

"Okay."

"We recommend you read these parenting books."

"Done."

This wasn't just about "fixing Amaya." This was about fixing our family, a concept that had never been thoroughly examined at the over-burdened and under-staffed Symphony Healthcare. And in regards to Amaya's father, grandmother, grandfather, uncles, aunt, and friends, they are (or were) going to do whatever they were going to do. How do you move forward, focusing on yourself, and go on to be a happy and productive person?

"And we'd like to run some psychological tests on Amaya."

"Of course."

Was I worried Amaya was bipolar? Yes, but only worried how others would look at her. Not so much worried about the diagnosis itself as I had seen Angela and Luke deal with the diagnosis since they were teens. "One more thing before you say your goodbyes. Try to let Amaya stand on-her-own here. Maybe write a letter to her every other day, not every day," I was told.

Now that Amaya was in a different state, I was only able to talk to her a few minutes a night, and although I drove the six hours there and back to visit weekly, visiting days and times were limited as well. Still, I did what was asked because I just wanted my daughter to be okay.

Gregg visited every other week, sometimes working a full day and then driving to California. He was able to attend a family therapy session or two in person, and the other times he was on speakerphone while I sat with Amaya. In a few short years, Gregg had proven over and over again that he was there for Amaya. Overtime, she started to refer to him not as her stepdad, but her dad. I love this!

As married couples do, Travis and I had conversations about death. "Just make sure you find someone who treats Amaya like she deserves to be treated," he would say. I knew I would wait for someone who treated Amaya well, but Gregg is beyond anything I could have dreamed of. Agnes and company knew Amaya was in California and why. My sister confirmed this. Again, not a call, not a text, not a card.

As a sober adult, Angela will tell you that she believes she was misdiagnosed with bipolar disorder as a teen. Luke too. I saw severe depression, like Amaya, in both of my siblings but I never saw severe swings in energy levels and mood (until my sister started doing drugs). Was it easier for our mother to hear the bipolar diagnosis and just fill a prescription every month than to get a second opinion? Was it easier for her to say, "Oh well, they are bipolar" when Angela and Luke acted out rather than really start addressing any issues that were causing their depression?

Amaya's test showed she was not bipolar either but to retest at a later age if I felt it was necessary. She was diagnosed with severe depression (in remission during the later part of treatment) and anxiety. She came home after forty-four days stronger than ever. I'm not saying every day has been easy. Getting her on the right combination of medications to help with her depression, anxiety, and sleep issues took some time. Dr. Still played an instrumental role in this.

Amaya has been free from purging since February 5, 2015 and has not tried to commit suicide since she threatened to jump off that mountain. No mother should have a lump in her throat every morning she goes to wake up her kid, worrying what she'll find. I don't worry as much anymore. I'll always worry to some degree as my daughter suffers from depression, that doesn't just go away. I do have to trust her to ask for help when she needs it. I had to learn that, to trust her.

Not every day is perfect in recovery, but we have learned communication skills that we use every day. I also try to be more patient and understanding toward Amaya than I was before, and I try not to take any of it personally. Mother-daughter relationships are never easy, but we work at it. It helps that there is mutual respect there.

Amaya wrote this on June 14, 2016 and with her permission, I am sharing it.

When I was in the 4th grade, I remember making myself throw up, not because I wanted to be skinny, I just didn't want to go to school that day. I remember raising my hand in 5th grade to use the restroom. I crouched in front of the toilet, I only felt pretty when I had nothing in my stomach. I washed my hands, drank some water, and went back to class like nothing happened. In 6th grade, someone heard me dry heaving, hunched over the toilet. I told them lunch didn't sit well.

In 7th grade, I pushed my lunch away. "I'll eat later," I said. I was lying. In 8th grade I wouldnt drink anything with calories or eat anything without throwing up. Until January, which is when I reached my breaking point.

# Fifteen

# Discoveries

I'm still in therapy. I started seeing a lady named Kathy once Destinations asked me to go back to therapy. The other lady I saw who asked me to write those letters to Tommy and Luke, I only saw a handful of times. She started a conversation I needed to have with myself, and I'm thankful for that, but Kathy I really like. When it relates to something I'm sharing with her, she shares bits of her life experiences with me, which I appreciate.

"I read something online. I think Agnes is a narcissist," I commented.

"You don't say," Kathy rolled her eyes.

"All of these statements apply to her, just listen...

*A narcissistic parent is envious and in competition with their child* - People have been telling me Agnes is jealous of me for years. Look how she acted when we got our home or when Gregg gave me his RAV4.

*Narcissists are all about appearances. Some may offer to loan you money, do not accept! It will be used against you at a later date* - Agnes is all about how she appears to others, and

I told you that any money you borrow comes with this unspoken loyalty to her.

*When meeting a narcissist for the first time, they often come across as extremely likeable* - Everyone loves Agnes when they first meet her.

*Narcissists are extremely selfish* - Mom has always put herself before her children.

*Narcissistic comments often hit below the belt* - She's told me she hated me, called me a bad mother, and said I was pathetic.

*Narcissists don't do therapy* - Hello! She wouldn't go with my sister and then Amaya.

*Narcissists never take responsibility for their actions or behavior* - Agnes has been denying the fact that she is an alcoholic for as long as I can remember, same with her gambling.

*Narcissistic parents create sibling rivalry and pit children against each other* - Look at what she's done to my brothers and me.

*The child who is the conformer is the golden child. They are taught to defend the parent. They are programmed to do what the parent wants* - This is Tommy and Luke.

*The rebel fights against the programming. The rebel receives constant belittling and criticism from the parent due to their lack of conforming* - This is Angela and me.

*The runner, they get as far away from the parent as possible -* This is us too. I could go on and on," I said.

Kathy laughed, "Again, this is not news to me. You grew up in an extremely dysfunctional alcoholic home."

I continued, "I'd also like to talk to you about my weight. I've told Amaya I felt my eating issues played a role in her eating disorder. She assures me I was a good role model, meaning that when I did lose weight, I did it the healthy way. True, but I still feel my constant up and down weight has, in fact, influenced her in some capacity. Amaya then told me Agnes used to call her chubby and encouraged her to try on bigger clothing sizes. I never knew this or I would have said something," I cried.

Going back to Agnes being a narcissist, I also read that whatever gift you buy for a narcissist is never good enough. This struck a cord too. Once Angela bought Agnes a chocolate brown leather jacket. Agnes opened the gift and said, "I wanted a black one." Years later, I got Agnes and Lorenzo a $50.00 gift card for Omaha Steaks. She complained that with *only* $50.00, she had to pay the shipping.

The very first time I ever remember fighting with Agnes (I don't refer to her as Mom so much nowadays), was over the lyrics to a Michael Jackson song. I was eight and we were stretching, getting ready to do aerobics. "What's the lyric?" Agnes asked as we touched our toes.

"The kid is not my son." I was certain.

"No, it's not."

"Yes, it is."

It was.

I tell this story because it involves exercise. Although I am 100% responsible for everything I have ever put in my mouth as an adult, I do wish proper nutrition was better explained and implemented to me as a child. Agnes briefly had that aerobics studio in the 80's, but other than an occasional workout tape we did together back then, once we moved to Vegas, I never saw Agnes work out, so neither did I. She stayed skinny by hardly eating, not exercising.

I don't know many stories from my mom's childhood because she hardly offered any. In one of the stories I do know, as a teen she went on an apple diet in which she would only eat, well, apples, and her hair started to fall out. Ba-Ba was always worried about Agnes' weight too, up until the day she died. Always asking her if she ate enough, or telling others she wished she would eat more.

Agnes told me to stay away from drugs, and for the most part I did. Would I have struggled with my weight my adult life if she had been just as passionate about diet, and staying active as trying to keep me off drugs? I wonder. Maybe I still would have destroyed my body, as I was hurting inside.

As of today, I've lost over twenty-five more pounds and counting. Once you've been obese and lose a lot of weight, you have extra skin. Real life isn't like *The Biggest Loser*. I'll forever have an apron of skin below my tummy, and I'll always have wings under my arms. Amaya has scars from cutting. My scars for abusing my body are my apron and wings.

When you are fat, you are seen and laughed at, but you are also invisible. I think I wanted to be invisible because I didn't feel worthy or good enough. Do I still think I'm garbage and that is why I would eat garbage? No, because in my forties, I am finally learning to love myself. It is a process.

On February 8, 2016, I reconnected with my stepsister on Facebook. I was nervous about also reconnecting with my biological father, but open to the idea. In some cases, time does help heal wounds. My stepmother was cautious at first, which I get now that I am older. She was just protecting her husband. Once she saw I wasn't after anything but a possible relationship with my father, she lowered her guard.

"I called you in 2007. Travis left you a message." I told my father.

"I know. I called Travis back, but he quickly asked me for money, and that was a red flag." *He called back and Travis had never told me? My dad could have possibly been in my life again nine years ago? Fuck you, Travis.*

I brought up my wedding to Brett. "I'd still have Pop-Pop walk me down the aisle, but I should have spoken to you about it beforehand. Maybe have you both do it. About that letter, calling Mom and me lesbians, that was hurtful." We both made apologies to each other, my stepmother too.

When I was eighteen and visited my dad, I did not ask him many of the questions I wanted to. I wasn't going to make that mistake again. "Dad, did you touch me? Bite me? Throw pots and pans at me?"

"Of course not, you should talk to some of your family members that knew us all back then." His voice was steady.

"I should have done that along time ago, I will definitely do that soon. Can I ask you about going to court with Mom?"

"Your mother tried to tell the judge I wasn't paying child support, yet I had all the receipts. "

*I was told my father never paid a dime.*

"I would come to your door every weekend, but your mother would always say you were sick."

*I grew up feeling my dad just didn't care to see me, and rarely tried too.*

"The judge ordered your mother to drop you off at a McDonald's so that I could see you. That's when she took off to Las Vegas."

The missing pieces were now falling into place. I only wrote about what I can remember of my young childhood. Seems I blocked much of it out. Why?

"Did you know your mother took off for a few months when you were two?"

"No. I didn't." Tears silently streamed down my face.

"Ba-Ba and Pop-Pop would come over every day to see you, asking me if I had heard from their daughter."

"I don't remember," I said robotically. *Ba-Ba and Pop-Pop knew? Agnes has called me a bad mom, yet she took off when I was two?*

"Yes, and my mother, your other grandmother, watched you while I worked. I took Agnes back because you needed your mother, and you cried for her every day she was gone. She then said she couldn't spend all day with you, so she got a part-time job and that's where she met Thomas. A few months later, she took off again, and this time she took you with her."

I was told my entire life that Thomas "saved" Agnes and me from my abusive father. I then spoke to several family members who knew Mom, Dad, and me back then and they all vouched for my father. They didn't know what I was told growing up, so no one sought me out to tell me anything. As a child, you believe your mother, so I wasn't asking questions back then either.

Of course I checked the facts. I didn't want any of this to be true. My life was much easier when I believed the biological father that I hardly knew was the bad guy.

My head was spinning. I became overwhelmed. I was learning bombshell after bombshell about my young life. Agnes had texted me in January 2016 on my birthday. No contact from her in over two years and she texts me a simple "Happy Birthday."

We had plans to attend a huge family reunion in the fall. She got wind of this and was simply trying to make nice beforehand. I've missed too many weddings and family reunions trying to avoid my mother. Not anymore. They are my family too.

I did not reply on my birthday but this was all way too much so I broke and sent this text on 2/28/2016:

Cher: Is there a reason you neglected to tell me you left me with my father when I was two, and just took off? If he was abusing me or biting me or throwing pots and pans at me, one would think you may not want to leave me with him...

See, he never did those things to me. Which has now been verified by many.

You lied to me, my entire life. You ran because that's what you do.

Sam cheats on you, run. Thomas cheats on you, run. My dad wants to see me more? Fuck him and run, and let's use Cher as a scapegoat, and fill her young mind with lies so she is afraid to ever ask questions.

The many secrets/lies you have, they have all been exposed. You are a selfish kidnapping liar and don't deserve the title of mother.

When people ask you how many kids you have, keep my name out of your mouth.

At the reunion, do not attempt to talk to me, Gregg, or Amaya. We will be civil, but know we want nothing to do with you.

Her reply was quick and it shattered my heart.

Agnes: Ha, you are funny. I'll give you that.

Cher: Nothing about this is funny Agnes, but your reply speaks volumes so thanks.

A few days went by and then I got this. I didn't even dignify it with a reply.

Agnes: I was advised today to issue a clear request that you refrain from sending any further harassment through my personal cell phone. I have expressed that I feel you are unstable and fear for my safety. As I am over 60 years of age I am protected by the state.

I was upset at Ba-Ba and Pop-Pop for a few days. How could they not tell me my own mother took off like that? Then I thought of Amaya. What if she did the same, but came back? What good would it do to tell my young grandchild? I believe my grandparents thought my mom and I were being abused, as that's the story Agnes told. It was more socially acceptable back in the late 70's to say you were abused and divorcing verses you committed adultery and were divorcing.

Dad and I talk just about every week. We look ahead instead of behind us. He made peace with what happened a long time ago. I'm working on it. We are making plans to reunite in person in 2017.

We lost well over twenty years. Being a narcissistic alcoholic and gambling addict is one thing, but I can never forgive Agnes for this. Growing up with your father is important. She robbed me of that. After I learned the truth, I did talk to my father and others regarding possible charges against Agnes. In the end, I decided not to pursue it for a few reasons. One of them being the unnecessary stress this situation would put on me in court and how that could affect my health.

When Cameron died and Amaya asked me why, I didn't have an answer then. But after a few months, I did. He died so both Amaya and I could find out we had Factor V Leiden Mutation, and take the precautions needed. Travis was always telling me that Amaya and I would be better off without him. Guess what? If he was going to remain in active addiction, we are better off. Gregg works hard to provide a wonderful life for Amaya and me. Loving Gregg is so easy too. He's the best husband I have ever had. Gregg loves that joke.

Like I wrote to my brothers, Mom has absolutely positively done some wonderful things for me. There are even a few parenting rules of hers that I have passed on. I couldn't have cotton candy as a child and I wouldn't allow Amaya to have it either. "It's pure sugar," Agnes would say. I couldn't play with fireworks, Amaya couldn't touch them until she was fifteen.

"New Year's Eve is for adults," was another saying of my mothers. Amaya stays home while I go to dinner with Gregg. But unlike Agnes, who has always partied the night away, I'm usually asleep well before the ball drops.

On a recent visit, Sue helped me discover why I always have my blinds closed and windows locked, just like my mom did when I was growing up in Vegas. "You don't have to hide like Agnes did. You didn't kidnap anyone," Sue encouraged me. She's right. I don't have to hide. Or be silent.

Mom has also done and said many horrific things. I wish I could go back and tell my ten-year-old self that you are good enough. Don't abuse your body like you will grow up to do. None of this is your fault, and one day you will learn the truth, and your eyes will be opened. You don't have to associate with anyone who hurts you, blood or not. Sometimes you may make the choice to forgive, and sometimes you don't have to keep trying when the other person does nothing to change. Sometimes you have to be your own biggest fan and never rely on anyone, but yourself, to pick yourself up and keep going.

I mailed one of the earliest drafts of this book to Catherine and Thomas. If I was writing a book about my life, their disownment of me obviously had a huge impact. I value the relationship I have now with them, and I was worried my memoir could derail it. Still, I mailed off my awful first draft, and proceeded to not sleep well for the next few weeks until Catherine and I set up a time to talk about what I had written.

"Are you guys mad at me?" I asked. Suddenly I was sixteen again.

"No, we are not mad at you. We understand you wrote what you did through the eyes of a child, but I need to explain something to you. When your mother took off with you and Tommy, her actions didn't just affect you." Catherine pointed out.

She went on, "If you felt resentment, you were right. We did resent you and your mother. Agnes had been putting us through hell for a very long time, and when it came to you, we didn't have to put up with it. When you were sixteen, we just decided not to deal with the bullshit anymore, from you or her. Looking back, could we have handled the situation differently? Yes."

I felt validated that she admitted I was treated differently, and I appreciated her honesty.

"Maybe you could have sat down with me at sixteen and tried to talk to me," I added.

"Perhaps. Thomas did talk to your mother at the time about this. Her response was that you didn't need us in your life anymore anyway."

*What? When I was sixteen, I'd cry to Agnes often about Thomas. She acted just as surprised as I was that I was disowned.*

I don't think Agnes will ever get sober or stop gambling. Not with enablers like Lorenzo, Tommy, and Luke near by. She'd have to take a good look in the mirror and admit all she has done. She'll never be ready to do that. In recent years, I've had more pity for her than anger. Thanks, therapy! I needed to write this book, to get this all out of my heart so I can stop reliving the past and continue my healing process. In showing my scars, maybe I can also help someone heal theirs.

I'm pretty awesome, so is my daughter, and Agnes hasn't known either of us for years. When it comes to Amaya, Agnes lies and says, "I don't get to see her much." She does not see her at all and she is at fault as to why. Amaya decided on her own not to have anything to do with her, especially after Agnes flat out refused to go to therapy with her. I will not deny that subconsciously Amaya may look to me and follow my lead.

I hate Mother's Day. I have accepted that I cannot have a relationship with my mother, but that doesn't mean it doesn't suck. Your mom is supposed to be your biggest fan and support you. Mother's Day is just a reminder of what I don't have. Of course Gregg and Amaya make sure to make me feel extra special on that day, but in part, Mother's Day is also about reflecting on your own mother.

I don't obsess over Agnes or my brothers like I used to. I would think about them and be so angry every day that I had to ask God to remove that obsessiveness from me and, with time, He did. Don't get me wrong. I miss my brothers every single day. It breaks my heart that I don't have a relationship with them. But at this time, I can't, and I have to make peace with it for my own happiness.

# Epilogue

I decided on the title of this book for quite a few reasons. Most should be pretty obvious at this point but in part, when I tell people that I have multiple sclerosis, I am very often met with, "But you look so good." MS is known as an iceberg disease. Although I, at times have been bedridden or unable to wash my own hair, I am blessed in the sense that my MS has been kinder to me than to some others. But know there is so much going on below the surface that you can't see. I've also been able to conceal my weight issues behind a pair of fat-hiding Spanx, carefully cropped photos, and a really good filter.

Although I played with the idea of dedicating this book to Agnes, in the end, I couldn't bring myself to give her that honor. But I do have to thank her. Thank you, Agnes, for lying to me, kidnapping me (and Tommy), and taking us to Las Vegas. Had you not, I would have never met Travis and therefore, there would be no Amaya. I believe Travis was in my life to teach me many lessons and to give me Amaya.

Speaking of Amaya, when I started writing this book, she had just gotten her learners permit. I blinked, and now she's sixteen. Amaya does very well in her honors courses, and is extremely focused and responsible. She is also the bravest person I know. Although, I do feel I failed her at times when Travis was still alive, my goal as her mother is to have Amaya look back and always say, "My mom put me first."

CPSIA information can be obtained
at www.ICGtesting.com
Printed in the USA
LVOW10s0028110717
540827LV00035B/1542/P